Iraq War

RODNEY P. CARLISLE

JOHN S. BOWMAN
GENERAL EDITOR

☑®
Facts On File, Inc.

Iraq War

Facts On File, Inc.
132 West 31st Street
New York NY 10001

Library of Congress Cataloging-in-Publication Data

Carlisle, Rodney P.
Iraq War / Rodney P. Carlisle.
p. cm. — (America at war)
Includes bibliographical references and index.
ISBN 0-8160-5627-7
1. Iraq War, 2003. 2. Iraq. I. Title. II. Series.
DS79.76.C363 2004
956.7044'3—dc22   2004005470

Facts On File books are available at special discounts when purchased in bulk quantities for businesses, associations, institutions, or sales promotions. Please call our Special Sales Department in New York at (212) 967-8800 or (800) 322-8755.

You can find Facts On File on the World Wide Web at http://www.factsonfile.com

Text design by Erika K. Arroyo
Logo design by Smart Graphics
Maps by Jeremy Eagle and Patricia Meschino

Printed in the United States of America

MP FOF 10 9 8 7 6 5 4 3 2 1

This book is printed on acid-free paper.

For Loretta, who
heard it all

Contents

Preface

Following the Persian Gulf War of 1990–91, the Iraqi regime of Saddam Hussein continued to defy the United Nations. His government made it nearly impossible for UN-appointed inspectors to determine whether Iraq had eliminated its programs to manufacture and deploy weapons of mass destruction (WMDs), including poison gas, biological agents that cause disease, and nuclear weapons. Although hampered in their work, UN inspectors did discover much evidence that these programs still existed. Some of the weapons were destroyed under UN supervision; however, by 1998 the United Nations withdrew its inspectors because it was clear that Hussein would not allow them free and unimpeded access to suspected sites. Furthermore, it appeared that he continued to conceal such programs.

On September 11, 2001 (9/11), the United States suffered the worst terrorist attack in its history, with the death of almost 3,000 victims in New York City, at the Pentagon near Washington, D.C., and at the site of a plane crash in Pennsylvania. President George W. Bush vowed that the perpetrators of these crimes would be brought to justice, or that justice would be brought to them. Consequently, in 2001–02 the United States conducted a rapid war in Afghanistan that destroyed the Taliban regime, a government that had harbored the al-Qaeda terrorist network and its members who planned and organized the 9/11 attacks. The continued defiance of the United Nations by the regime of Hussein convinced both President Bush of the United States and Prime Minister Tony Blair of Great Britain that Hussein's regime represented a major threat to world order. They argued that his brutal and cynical regime, which had a long record of financing and supporting terrorists, might soon make its advanced weapons, training facilities, funding, and WMDs available to the surviving remnants of the al-Qaeda organization.

Through the early months of 2003, both Bush and Blair sought to convince their legislatures and the leaders of allied nations that force should be used against Iraq to eliminate the threats represented by the Iraqi regime. Sharing some information gathered from intelligence operations, both leaders received the consent of their legislatures to proceed against Iraq, but with few exceptions, traditional allies such as Canada, France, and Germany refused to support such action. The UN Security Council and the North Atlantic Treaty Organization (NATO) both declined to offer official support for a U.S. and British military action against Iraq.

In a dramatic three-week campaign beginning March 20, 2003, U.S. and British forces (together with nominal support from several other countries in a coalition), destroyed the Iraqi army, defeating the regime of Saddam Hussein. Hussein himself evaded death or capture at that time, and his government offered no formal surrender. As U.S. troops pushed into Baghdad, the country's capital, Iraqi soldiers simply took off their uniforms and went home. Without surrender and with no for-

After the defeat of the Iraqi army, an uneasy peace descended on Baghdad, as observed in late April 2003 by troops aboard this HH-60 helicopter from the 301st Rescue Squadron of the U.S. Air Force. *(Staff Sergeant Cherie A. Thurlby, Department of Defense)*

mal government left in the country, a period of looting and sporadic resistance to the occupying forces set in. Over the next months, it became clear that former members of the Iraqi regime, together with some armed anti-American forces from outside Iraq, had started a long and bitter armed resistance. Although the war itself had been conducted with less than 120 Americans killed in action prior to Bush's May 1 declaration of the end of combat, deaths among occupying American troops after May 1 had already exceeded that number by fall 2003.

In many ways, the Iraq War of 2003 was unique. Although an extremely successful war by the common measures of duration of conflict and casualties incurred by U.S. troops, it ranked as one of the most controversial in American history. From the beginning, polls indicated that a clear majority of the American people supported the president in his decisions, but a vociferous and articulate minority continued to debate many issues. Central among those issues were whether the war was justified, whether the methods used in the war were appropriate, and whether the planning for the postwar "endgame" was well thought out.

Some of the problems raised in connection with the Iraq War of 2003, known officially as Operation Iraqi Freedom, are among the most important today. Many of them may be debated in public for years to come. It is important that students—and for that matter, the general public—recognize that such crucial problems can be discussed intelligently against a background of information, as well as against a background of conflicting values. All too often, "informed opinion" is absent in the media, with discussions reflecting heat, not light. This work has been carefully crafted to assist readers in weighing the merits of differing viewpoints about serious policy questions.

This work begins with the "shock and awe" campaign that marked the start of the war. Americans were perhaps as awed as the residents of Baghdad as they viewed the spectacular detonations broadcast from that city over television worldwide on March 20, 2003. To understand what lay behind that attack, the following chapters backtrack, exploring pertinent aspects of Iraqi and Middle Eastern history, the first war in the Persian Gulf, and the problem of determining whether the Hussein regime continued to develop WMDs. The book then traces the 2003 war itself, records the reaction of the public in the United States and around the world, and explores the tangled aftermath of the war.

Operation Iraqi Freedom and the larger "war on terror" conducted around the world since September 11, 2001, have led to deeply divisive debates over a great many issues. Among those considered in this book are the following:

1. The contrast between the Persian Gulf War and the Iraq War: Why was there so little international debate in 1990 and so much in 2003? Why was there so much domestic debate in 2003?
2. Was the Iraq War a just war?
3. Did President George W. Bush establish a dangerous precedent with a doctrine of "preemptive war"?
4. Did President George W. Bush and Prime Minister Tony Blair mislead their legislatures and their peoples about the WMD threat?
5. Why did the "inspection regime" not work out?
6. Why did some long-standing U.S. allies, such as France, Canada, and Mexico, disagree with the American decision to go to war against Iraq?
7. Could the Iraqi regime under Saddam Hussein be considered a modern state? Are comparisons of Hussein to Adolf Hitler justified?
8. Is the world safer from terrorists after the Iraq War?
9. Why was it so much harder to establish peace in Iraq than it was in Japan, Germany, and Italy after World War II?
10. How could the war against such an apparently powerful Iraqi enemy be conducted with so few coalition casualties? Was the rapid victory due to lack of resolve by the Iraqis or to superior U.S. war-fighting technology and training?
11. Why were American military experts' comments for the media so wrong about the duration and the difficulty of the war?
12. Did the U.S. government and military really do all they could to limit civilian casualties? Did such control hamper the U.S. effort?
13. Did the American and international news media report independently or were they co-opted by the process of being "embedded" with the troops?

These and other issues about the war have no simple answers; however, informed discussion about these controversies is possible and is preferable to simple disagreement or uninformed argument. Issues sometimes get reduced to angry name-calling, with charges of war-mongering on one side and disloyalty to the American cause on the other side, rather than a weighing of the facts and the principles. This work presents factual material in a balanced way so that readers can draw their own conclusions and weigh the arguments on both sides.

PREFACE

Some passages simply let the narrative convey the facts that illuminate the multiple sides and shadings of a complex debate. The reader will learn that the legacy of the Iraq War of 2003 has been a set of controversies that resemble yet go beyond those of the Persian Gulf War of 1991.

Every chapter has at least one boxed topic that explores related issues in greater depth. Illustrations and maps provide a further dimension to the subject matter. This book also provides definitions, dates, facts, and information in straightforward language, while a glossary of terms at the end of the book provides definitions for continual and handy reference. A final section lists sources of further information, both in printed and electronic form.

As this book goes to press in 2004, only now are other historical treatments of the Iraq War being published, and no doubt there will be many more in future years. Many of the open issues left unresolved in the aftermath of the war may yet be resolved with interrogation of high-ranking members of the former Iraqi regime. So the student of this topic who consults this work in future years should be aware that more recent information may further illuminate some of the questions raised here.

1

SHOCK AND AWE

Although the world was braced for a campaign of "shock and awe" bombing of Baghdad, the capital of Iraq, events moved quickly on Wednesday, March 19, 2003. It was 7:15 P.M. in Washington D.C., and 3:15 Thursday morning, March 20 in Baghdad. In Washington, at the end of a three-hour meeting, President George W. Bush gave the order: "Let's go."

In Baghdad, television cameras picked up the night sky full of tracer bullets and the shriek of air-raid sirens as Iraqi air defenses harmlessly sought out attacking American F-117 aircraft. At about 3:30 A.M., the planes dropped heavy 2,000-pound "bunker-buster" bombs on a private residence outside the city, and nearly simultaneously, some 40 Tomahawk cruise missiles slammed into command facilities near the building. American intelligence officials had learned that Iraqi president Saddam Hussein might be in a deeply concealed shelter beneath the building.

The Iraq War of 2003 had begun, some 45 minutes before the expiration of a deadline: President Bush had given Hussein 48 hours to resign and leave the country; Hussein had rejected the ultimatum earlier that day. U.S. secretary of defense Donald Rumsfeld told reporters that if Hussein rejected the ultimatum, the United States could attack at any time after the rejection. Characteristically, Rumsfeld refused to be specific with reporters, and they could only guess when the first attack might take place. At 10:15 P.M. President Bush addressed the American people on television, announcing the beginning of Operation Iraqi Freedom.

After the initial raid, the city of Baghdad fell silent. Over the next day, news of unfolding events began to flow in a steady stream. To assure the world that he was still alive, Hussein appeared on television.

Commentators noticed he wore heavy glasses, seemed to lose his place in his handwritten notes more than once, and appeared shaken and hardly as confident and defiant as he had in recent speeches. Despite some suspicions that Hussein had been killed and the speech was given by a stand-in double, most analysts concluded that he had survived the attack.

After the initial predawn strikes in Baghdad, the city remained quiet until cruise missiles and bombs began to hit the Ministry of Planning around 9:00 P.M. local time. An hour earlier, the 1st Marine Expeditionary Force had begun moving into Iraq from Kuwait.

Observers were immediately struck by how different this war was from the Persian Gulf War of 1990–91. In the earlier war against Iraq, Coalition forces had relentlessly bombed air defenses and ground emplacements for a month prior to the first insertion of ground troops. This time, the troops moved in immediately, without an extended period to allow air power to soften up the defenses. Critics feared that this latter strategy would expose U.S. troops to a withering defense by the Iraqis. Other aspects of the unfolding strategy surprised military observers. In 1991, General Norman Schwarzkopf had commanded a coalition of more than 550,000 troops. In 2003, General Tommy Franks directed a force not exceeding 150,000 troops.

The coalitions themselves were quite different. In 1991, troops and pilots from Saudi Arabia, the Persian Gulf states, Egypt, Syria, France, and other countries had worked with Americans, Canadians, and British to expel Iraq from its invasion of Kuwait. Although President Bush announced in 2003 that some 40 nations offered their support in this second war against Iraq, only Britain, Australia, and the United States sent sizable military units, with a very small contingent from Poland. The Czech Republic offered to send a chemical warfare unit to help in decontaminating any chemical weapon residue but not to engage in combat. Spain provided a hospital ship but no troops. Most of the other countries in the 2003 coalition offered only political or moral support, and the list of 40 nations included some micro-countries that were politically and economically dependent on the United States, such as the Republic of the Marshall Islands.

Despite claims that the campaign would represent one of "shock and awe," the initial pinpoint-target air strikes on March 19, launched ahead of schedule, were hardly that impressive. Over the next week, air raids over Baghdad intensified. The thud of bombs and detonations were spectacular and awe-inspiring. Filmed from nearby hotels, the govern-

A War Fought in Two Time Zones

BECAUSE BAGHDAD IS ABOUT 120 DEGREES OF LONGI-
tude to the east of Washington, D.C., there is an eight-hour time difference between the two cities. When it is noon in Washington, it is
8:00 P.M. in Baghdad. The table shows the timing of key events as the
war began.

Washington, D.C. Date and Time (EST)	Baghdad, Iraq Date and Time
Wednesday, March 19	**Wednesday, March 19**
10:15 A.M.	6:15 P.M.
noon	8:00 P.M.
	Thursday, March 20
7:15 P.M.[a]	3:15 A.M.
8:00 P.M.[b]	4:00 A.M.
10:15 P.M.[c]	6:15 A.M.
Thursday, March 20	
noon	8:00 P.M.[d]
1:00 P.M.	9:00 P.M.[e]

[a] President George W. Bush orders raid on bunker at 7:12 P.M.; raid begins
about 7:15 P.M. Eastern standard time.
[b] Deadline officially ends after 48 hours.
[c] Bush addresses nation on TV; 15 minutes later, he learns that planes from first
raid are safely back.
[d] First Expeditionary Marines move into Iraq from Kuwait.
[e] Air raid hits Ministry of Planning and other government buildings.

ment compounds, ministries, and presidential palaces along the Tigris
River were set afire and reduced to rubble. However, the bombing campaign itself was quite different from that in the Persian Gulf War. This
time, pilots and missile-targeting crews were careful to select only identified military and political leadership targets, avoiding the destruction
of bridges, power stations, and other infrastructure. U.S. Defense
Department officials explained that there was no need to destroy such
facilities and by leaving them in place, the United States would not have
to fund their reconstruction after the war.

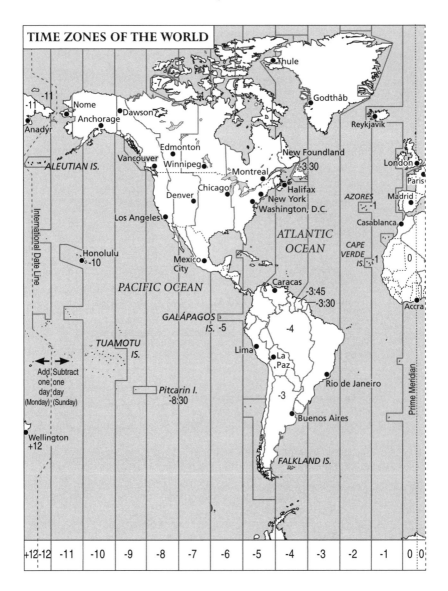

TIME ZONES OF THE WORLD

Military experts commenting for the news media were puzzled at these new strategies. Could a war be won without all-out destruction of the enemy's network of transportation facilities? How could a force less than half as strong as that mounted in 1991 be expected to conquer all of Iraq? After all, in 1991, more than 500,000 troops had a very limited

SHOCK AND AWE

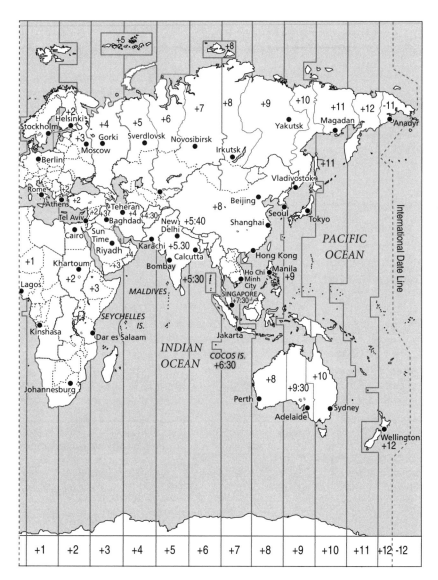

objective: the liberation of Kuwait. There was no need to move forces deep into Iraq in that war. However, in 2003, the troops not only would have to push back Iraqi defenders, they would need to conquer a much larger country and face what promised to be disastrous street-to-street, house-to-house battles in Baghdad itself.

The Origins of Shock and Awe

THE TERM *SHOCK AND AWE* IS DERIVED FROM A strategy paper developed in 1996 at the National Defense University by a team of strategists under the leadership of security analyst Harlan K. Ullman. Ullman and his team pointed out that in modern conflicts it would be important to instill in an attacked leadership a psychological sense of defeat, brought on by an overwhelming and powerful force applied so as to achieve "rapid dominance." In the report and in other documents, Ullman compared the concept to the employment of atomic weapons in 1945 against the cities of Hiroshima and Nagasaki in Japan. The stunning effect of those attacks induced the Japanese leadership to agree to surrender within a few days. Ullman pointed out that modern weapons such as cruise missiles, when directed against specific targets, including government facilities or crucial infrastructure, could rapidly demoralize an enemy.

At first, when the media picked up on the phrase *shock and awe* current in military circles, they were unaware of its origins. When the missile and bombing attacks did not have the immediate effect of bringing about surrender, commentators assumed the phrase was a form of bluster or propaganda. When the concept was traced to Ullman's 1996 report, critics of the war effort spelled out the parallels to the nuclear attacks of 1945 that Ullman himself had used. Some even used that parallel and its implicit technological arrogance to support their claims that the U.S. administration had adopted an unnecessarily aggressive policy. For most of the public, however, the phrase simply represented a convenient label for the heavy targeted bombardment of government offices and palaces in Iraq.

Analysts searched for reasons why the timetable of the new war had been sped up so. The military had received reports that there were fires around the Rumaila oil fields in southern Iraq. One of those fires was in a trench, apparently set to cloud over the battlefield and to provide protection for Iraqi forces from air strikes. In addition, at least another six oil wells seemed to be on fire. Word leaked out that the timing of the ground attack had been pushed ahead by at least a week, partly because the air raids on Baghdad intended to target Hussein himself. Iraqis had started to lob missiles at U.S. and British troops who were poised to attack from Kuwait. In Kuwait, loudspeakers blared, "This is not a drill," as Iraqi missiles exploded within 600 yards of Camp Commando, a main camp of U.S. ground forces. One missile was identified as a Chinese-made Seersucker antiship missile, and two others were thought to be Iraqi Ababil-100 surface-to-surface missiles. With American troops facing possible chemical warfare assaults from such missiles, U.S. generals conferred by secured video-conferencing lines and decided to move in.

U.S. Marines cut slits in the protective sand berms (raised banks) and filled in some of the tank ditches, moving forward in coordinated attacks. The U.S. Army's 3rd Infantry Division, some 20,000 troops, began pouring into Iraq, meeting only light resistance. Iraqi guards abandoned their border posts. There were no American battle casualties in these first advances, although a helicopter accident on March 20 claimed the lives of 16 American marines and British royal commandos.

Meanwhile, key units of the Iraqi defenders were hit by coordinated attacks from helicopter gunships, cruise missiles, and army long-distance surface-to-surface missiles. Targets ranged from positions on Safwan Hill, a 440-foot-high spot just inside the Iraqi border, to encampments and

The FA-18 Hornet, equipped with sophisticated electronic systems, was capable of precise aiming at military targets, thereby leaving much of Iraq's infrastructure undamaged. (Lieutenant J. G. Perry Solomon, Department of Defense)

Soldiers of the 3rd Infantry Division set up a perimeter defense on March 24, 2003, during their advance through southern Iraq. *(Sergeant Igor Paustovski, Department of Defense)*

headquarters further north. In the first day of battle, Republican Guard headquarters in Kirkuk in northern Iraq was targeted, as were regular Iraqi army units in An Nasiriyah and at other locations between the Kuwait border and Baghdad.

Another difference between the war launched in 2003 and that fought in 1991 was the reaction of the general public and leadership around the world and in the United States. Whereas in 1990–91 a broad coalition was built, in 2003, very little international support was forthcoming. In Germany, Chancellor Gerhard Schröder stated that Bush's decision to go to war was wrong; Jacques Chirac, president of France, took an equally hard stand. In Russia and China, leaders appealed to American leadership to allow a political, not military solution. In Rome and Athens, tens of thousands of protesters marched against the attack on Iraq. In Canada, Prime Minister Jean Chrétien reiterated Canadian opposition to the war, although he did comment that nothing should be done to comfort Hussein. Indications of support, but no ground troops came from Spain, Japan, South Korea, and the Philippines. Pope John Paul II said that he was "deeply pained" that Hussein had not accepted the United Nations resolutions requiring cooperation with inspectors, but he also criticized the United States for not continuing negotiations.

In the United States, polls continued to show that a majority supported the president's actions, but the support was clearly not universal. Indeed, some of the minority opponents were vocal and very angry. In the first week of the war, about 100 protesters were arrested in Philadelphia, eight more in Los Angeles, and 21 in New York City. San Francisco saw the largest demonstration in the United States, with about 1,000 protesters arrested in the financial district. Marchers in that city attempted to disrupt traffic at intersections. In various protests elsewhere, some students walked out of classes, and small groups gathered in public spots in cities from Bangor, Maine, to Nacogdoches, Texas. In scattered locations, some protesters attempted to block traffic or close down businesses.

Many factors had contributed to the worldwide disagreement and American public division over whether this war was appropriate. For most Americans, however, the memories of the terrorist attacks of September 11, 2001, had left a residue of anger, and their support for a war on terror extended to support for the president and for the troops in Iraq.

2

THE MIDDLE EAST SITUATION

According to a joke that circulated during the months leading up to the 2003 invasion of Iraq, Mohammed Aldouri, the Iraqi ambassador to the United Nations, told Colin Powell, U.S. secretary of state, "I understand that only 10 percent of American high school graduates know where Iraq is." Powell replied, "That's true. Unfortunately for you, they're all U.S. Marines!" Of course, as the situation in the Middle East became more serious, more and more Americans learned not only the geography of the region but also a lot about the history that had led up to the crisis.

The region between the Tigris and Euphrates Rivers, in the heart of modern-day Iraq, was known as Mesopotamia. Dubbed "the cradle of civilization," Mesopotamia is where human beings first developed agriculture, invented the wheel and writing, and built the first cities about 6,000 years ago. In ancient times, empires based in one or another Mesopotamian city—Ur, Babylon, Nineveh—flourished and spread their power and their knowledge of metalworking, domestication of plants and animals, and other skills in all directions. The peoples of the Mediterranean such as the Greeks learned the skills of civilization from the Mesopotamians.

By the year 1910, Mesopotamia and its surrounding deserts and mountains were the easternmost province of the Ottoman Empire, whose capital was Constantinople, in Turkey. Like other empires, the Ottoman Empire consisted of many different nations, religions, and ethnic groups. The peoples of the Ottoman Empire spoke numerous languages, including several dialects of Arabic, as well as Kurdish, Turkish, Greek, Armenian, and other languages. A majority of the peoples in the empire were Muslims, with pockets (and some larger regions) populated by Christians and other religions scattered through the diverse empire.

The word *Islam* in the Arabic language means "submission," that is, submission to the will of God, and it is the name of the religion founded

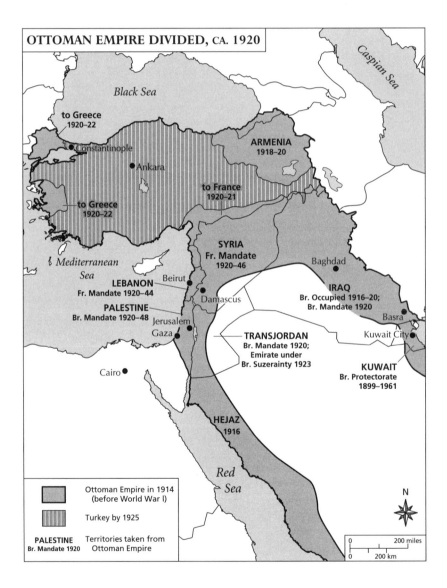

OTTOMAN EMPIRE DIVIDED, CA. 1920

Black Sea

Caspian Sea

to Greece
1920–22

Constantinople

ARMENIA
1918–20

Ankara

to France
1920–21

to Greece
1920–22

Mediterranean Sea

SYRIA
Fr. Mandate
1920–46

Baghdad

LEBANON
Fr. Mandate 1920–44

Beirut

IRAQ
Br. Occupied 1916–20;
Br. Mandate 1920

Damascus

PALESTINE
Br. Mandate 1920–48

Jerusalem

Gaza

Basra

TRANSJORDAN
Br. Mandate 1920;
Emirate under
Br. Suzerainty 1923

Kuwait City

Cairo

KUWAIT
Br. Protectorate
1899–1961

HEJAZ
1916

Red Sea

N

Ottoman Empire in 1914
(before World War I)

Turkey by 1925

PALESTINE
Br. Mandate 1920

Territories taken from
Ottoman Empire

0   200 miles

0   200 km

THE MIDDLE EAST SITUATION

Muslims from all over the world gather annually for a pilgrimage to the shrine of the Kaaba (the sacred stone of Islam) in the courtyard of the Great Mosque in Mecca. *(Library of Congress, Prints and Photographs Division [LC-USZ62-99278])*

by Muhammad (ca. 570–632) and followed by Muslims. Muhammad was born in the Arabian city of Mecca, which is now regarded as the holiest city of Islam. Among Muslims, there are the Shiite and the Sunni, separate branches whose division goes back to a dispute between two lines of descendants of Muhammad. But for both branches of Islam, the Qur'an (Koran), a compilation of Muhammad's teachings, provides a guide to day-to-day life, ethics, and behavior, as well as to the practice of faith. The rules to proper behavior under Islam are known as the sharia, or "pathway." The Shiite believe that the sharia is strictly set forth by Muhammad in the Qur'an. By contrast, the Sunni also accept practices and rules that are endorsed universally by the faithful. The contrast may seem subtle, but it leads to many differences in day-to-day lifestyle between the Shiite and Sunni.

By accepting rules of behavior endorsed by the faithful, the Sunni are generally more open to changing practices and modern developments. For this reason, Sunni Muslims in general have adapted more comfortably to changes in clothing, lifestyle, and manners of the modern era. For example, more Sunni than Shiite find it acceptable that women should be able to receive higher education and hold professional positions and that they need not wear veils over their faces and hair in public.

Both Sunni and Shiite Muslims share many aspects of their faith and study the Qur'an. Divided into 114 chapters, or suras, the Qur'an is seen as divinely revealed to Muhammad. Basic to Islam are its five pillars of faith: recitation of the creed, worship in the direction of the city of Mecca, giving of alms or charity to the poor, fasting from dawn to sundown during the month of Ramadan (a month that is not fixed in the Western calendar), and making a pilgrimage to Mecca once during one's lifetime. Both Sunni and Shiite share belief in these five pillars, and during the annual pilgrimage to Mecca, Muslims of both branches from many countries, stretching from Morocco in northwest Africa to Indonesia, off the coast of Southeast Asia, meet and share devotion in Mecca. They are joined by other Muslims from North America and Europe, as the religion is a truly international and interracial world faith.

Of the two branches of Islam, the Shiites have emerged as the more conservative wing of the religion, in which the advice of religious leaders, or imams, is followed in everyday social, ethical, and political affairs. The Sunni Muslims are also devout but rely more on nonreligious figures such as kings, emirs, or presidents for day-to-day political leadership. Western observers often speak of *fundamentalist* Shiites and *moderate* Sunnis, using these terms much as they are applied to Christianity to draw a rough parallel to the differences between the two branches of Islam. In general it is true that Shiites tend to adhere to a more strictly "fundamental," or traditional, view of Islam; however, such generalizations can be deceptive, since many Sunni Muslims are very strict in their observance of rules laid out in the Qur'an.

The Islamic faith originated on the Arabian Peninsula and then spread by conquest and conversion westward across North Africa and eastward through central and southern Asia. The people of the different countries on the Arabian Peninsula are Arabs, and their language is Arabic. In the countries of North Africa from Egypt and Sudan west to Morocco, dialects of Arabic are the official language and are widely spoken. Ethnic Arabs make up about 75 percent of the population of Iraq, and Arabic is the official language there as well.

At its peak the Ottoman Empire had ruled a vast region including parts of southeastern Europe (into the area of Greece, Albania, and Kosovo), all of Turkey, the Arabian Peninsula, and Egypt. By 1910, that empire had shrunk but still ruled a broad sweep of land from Turkey through the Arabian Peninsula, the Persian Gulf, and east to Mesopotamia. During World War I (1914–18), the Ottoman Empire sided with Germany and the Austro-Hungarian Empire. Together, they were known as the Central Powers and fought against the Allies: Britain, France, Russia, Italy, and later, the United States. At the end of World War I, the victorious Allies broke up the empires of the Central Powers.

A crowd witnesses the signing of the Treaty of Versailles, June 28, 1919, formally bringing an end to World War I and rearranging the map of Europe and the Middle East. *(National Archives, Still Picture Branch, NWDNS-111-SC-159296)*

Independence of Former Ottoman Empire States

AT THE END OF WORLD WAR I, THE OTTOMAN EMPIRE was broken up. Turkey, which had been the ruling part of the empire, emerged as a modernizing republic under the dynamic leadership of Kemal Ataturk in 1923. Meanwhile, a more conservative regime, headed by King Ibn Saud, established Saudi Arabia out of two former Ottoman provinces, Nejd and Hejaz, in 1926. The rest of the former empire was governed by the British and French under the League of Nations mandate system. The two European powers turned over control to local regimes one by one, beginning with Jordan in 1923; Iraq, 1932; Lebanon, 1944; Syria, 1946; Israel, 1948; Kuwait, 1961; and the Persian Gulf States of Bahrain, Qatar, and the United Arab Emirates, 1971.

The Ottoman Empire was no longer. Turkey became a republic in 1923, and Arabia emerged as an independent kingdom in 1926. The Arab regions and provinces of the former empire, such as Iraq, Kuwait, Palestine, Lebanon, Syria, and smaller countries in the Persian Gulf, were administered as mandates or protectorates by Britain and France. Although not colonies, the mandates were run by administrators sent by Britain and France, much like colonies. The international League of Nations, which had set up the mandates, expected the European administrators to be in the region only for a temporary period and then turn over the mandates to local rule. The Arab peoples remembered this period with some resentment, as it seemed the Europeans were reluctant to leave. One by one, however, the British and French mandates were eventually converted to independent rule.

One reason that the British held on to the administration of Kuwait and the Persian Gulf States for so long was that they turned out to have rich oil reserves underground, discovered in the 1930s. As Americans, Europeans, and Asians bought automobiles (and trucks, aircraft, and petroleum-fueled ships) during the 1930s, the world demand for oil increased. Soon, the oil fields of the United States, Mexico, and Venezuela were supplemented by the rich new finds under the lands of Arabia, Iraq, Kuwait, and the Persian Gulf States (especially Qatar and

Bahrain). The crude oil was pumped from wells, then shipped by pipeline and tanker and delivered to refineries in Europe, the United States, and Japan.

Oil had made the region extremely important to the world economy in the space of 10 years. The British and American oil companies and governments kept a close watch on the countries of the region to ensure that the steady flow of oil was protected. During World War II (1939–45), one of the principal strategic aims of the United States and Britain was to ensure that Germany did not gain control of Arabia, the Persian Gulf, and Iraq.

Other issues added to the ethnic and religious complexity and to the oil economics, making the region a source of one conflict after another through the years following World War II. One such issue that remained almost constantly in the news for a half century was the situation in the former Ottoman province of Palestine.

When the British relinquished the Palestine mandate in 1948, they moved out, and Jewish settlers who had immigrated to the region over the past decades set up the State of Israel there. Jewish settlers had moved into Palestine during the last days of the Ottoman Empire, hoping to escape the persecution they faced in parts of Europe and planning to establish a homeland. Following World War I, the British had reluctantly allowed some immigration of European Jews into Palestine, and then following the Nazi extermination campaign against the Jews in the 1930s and 1940s, the flow of immigration increased by the tens of thousands. Palestinian Arabs and the Arabs in neighboring countries resented the British for letting in the European-born Jewish immigrants, and especially for turning over the lands to local Jewish authorities when they left in 1948 without having resolved territorial arrangements promised to the Palestinian Arabs under the mandate. In a short and bitter war, the new State of Israel fought against troops from Iraq, Jordan, Syria, and Egypt who sought to prevent the establishment of a Jewish, rather than a Muslim state in the region.

Israel won the war and began to receive financial and military aid from the United States; from thereon the existence of Israel was a sore issue for many Arabs in the Middle East. In 1956, 1967, and 1973 Israel fought other short wars, occupying more and more territories inhabited by Arabs, leading to further continuing disputes.

Meanwhile, the oil issue continued to make the area increasingly crucial to the United States, which had emerged from World War II as the dominant world power along with the Soviet Union. By the 1950s, the flow of oil from the Middle East to the United States became extremely important, because Americans had begun to burn more fuel than they produced from their own oil fields in Texas, California, and elsewhere in the country. America became a net importer of oil by the end of the 1950s, and the Middle East was crucial to that supply. Countries such as Iraq, Iran, and Saudi Arabia were suddenly much more important to the United States than they had been two decades before.

Iraq, as an independent country, included quite a diverse group of people, resembling on a smaller scale some of the diversity in the old Ottoman Empire. In the northern region of the country, Kurdish-speaking people, mostly Sunni Muslims, were a distinct ethnic minority. The Kurds had hoped that when the Ottoman Empire dissolved, they would receive an independent Kurdish nation. Instead, the League of Nations–drawn boundaries divided the Kurds between Iraq, Turkey, and

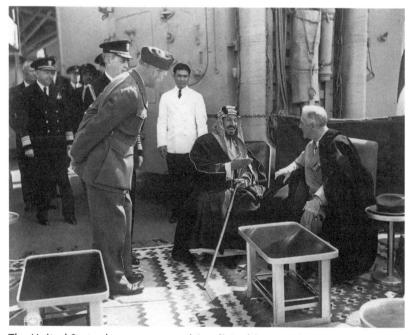

The United States began to regard Saudi Arabia as an important oil-supplying state as early as World War II. Here President Franklin Roosevelt meets with King Ibn Saud in Egypt. *(Franklin D. Roosevelt Presidential Library)*

Syria to the west and Iran to the east. There was to be no single Kurdistan. Scattered through the northern region of Iraq were also small pockets of Turkish-speaking Turkomans.

In the center of Iraq, Arabic-speaking Sunni peoples dominated in the capital city of Baghdad, along with smaller cities to the north and south of Baghdad. Further down the Tigris and Euphrates Rivers, including in the city of Basra and the port city of Umm Qasr on the Persian Gulf, Shiite Arabs were the majority. In numbers, there were about twice as many Shiites as Sunnis in all of Iraq.

To the east of Iraq, the country of Iran would play an important part in the history of Iraq. Iran was populated largely by non-Arab, Farsi-speaking people (known historically in Europe as Persians), who were mostly Shiite Muslims. In 1953, when a political crisis occurred under Iran's prime minister Mohammad Mosaddeq, who opposed the country's pro-British and pro-American shah (leader), the United States quietly supported a coup by the Iranian army, which overthrew Mosaddeq. From the 1950s onward, the United States strongly supported the shah with military and financial assistance, seeing his regime as a strong bulwark against the Communist Soviet Union to the north, as a reliable supplier of oil, and as a staunch ally in the region. For decades, the shah and his secret police ruled Iran, ensuring a flow of oil.

However, popular resentment toward the shah of Iran mounted, especially among the influential Shiite clergy in that country, and in 1979, the shah was overthrown. A religious leadership established a revolutionary Islamic state. A group of Americans in the U.S. embassy were seized and held hostage for more than a year in 1979–81.

Meanwhile, Saddam Hussein had emerged as the leader of neighboring Iraq in 1979. A Sunni Muslim, as nearly all his predecessors since the late 1950s had been, Hussein ruled his country through a combination of tight police control, terror, and the use of propaganda. When Shiites in the south of Iraq sought to imitate the new regime in Iran, Hussein used troops and police to round up religious leaders and execute them. Similarly, when Kurds in the north joined with Kurds in Iran to assert their independence, Hussein suppressed them as well. In the period 1980–88, Iran and Iraq fought a long and bitter war. Hussein began using medium-ranged missiles, some loaded with poison gas, as part of the weapons against the Iranians. He authorized the use of poison gas against Kurds in the town of Halabja in the north of Iraq, killing thousands and injuring thousands of others. This poison gassing of his own citizens shocked the

This injured Kurdish girl is carried to a waiting ambulance after arriving in Geneva, Switzerland. She was one of thousands of victims of a nerve gas attack ordered by Saddam Hussein on her village in 1988. *(D. Stampfli, AP/Wide World Photos)*

world. During the long war between Iraq and Iran, the United States provided Hussein with information and technical advice hoping he would bring to an end the strongly anti-American regime in Iran. However, the war ended in a stalemate, after the Iraqis had lost an estimated 120,000 citizens and suffered more than 300,000 wounded.

During the 1980s in the Iran-Iraq War, the Iranians often attacked oil tankers carrying Iraqi crude oil. The huge ships that carried oil from Iraq steamed down through the Persian Gulf past the shores of Iran, to refineries in Europe, America, and Japan, providing an easy target for the warships and aircraft of the Iranians. The Iraqis retaliated. Each side began using antiship missiles to destroy and sink fully loaded crude oil tankers, often causing casualties among the international crews of the ships and spreading oil pollution in the Persian Gulf.

This "Tanker War" threatened to spread. Kuwait, as a Sunni Arab state, provided financial aid to Hussein's Iraqi government during the Iran-Iraq War, so the Iranians decided to sink tankers carrying Kuwaiti crude oil. In order to protect some of those tanker ships, often destined to U.S. oil refineries, the American government allowed the owners to re-register several Kuwaiti tankers in the United States and then use U.S. naval ships for protection. When the tankers flew the American flag, and the U.S. Navy stood by, the Iranians avoided targeting the Kuwaiti oil.

Although Iraq had a strong army and many modern weapons, it also had incurred a massive multibillion dollar foreign debt over the 1980s, much of it owed to Saudi Arabia and to Kuwait for the aid that those countries had provided during the long war against Iran. At the end of that war, Hussein sought to get both Kuwait and Saudi Arabia to forgive the owed debt. He argued that the Iraqi army had sacrificed for all Sunni Arabs against the Shiite Farsi regime of Iran. He began to use demands for debt relief to threaten Kuwait by 1989 and 1990. All of these cross-currents of religion, geography, oil economics, and ethnic division help account for the position of Iraq in 1990.

3

SADDAM HUSSEIN, THE BAATH PARTY, AND WEAPONS OF MASS DESTRUCTION

Iraq became an independent monarchy in 1932, one of the first Middle Eastern mandates under the League of Nations to graduate from European armed protectorate status to independence. In 1958, a series of military governments took over from the monarchy. By 1979, Saddam Hussein emerged as the head of government, although he had exercised control from behind the scenes as early as 1968. Hussein began the war against neighboring Iran in 1980 and at the same time continued to operate his brutal and ruthless regime. Just as the earlier dictators Benito Mussolini in Italy and Adolf Hitler in Germany had worked through control of a dominant fascistic political party, Hussein used his control of the Iraqi Baath Party as a source of power.

Hussein had built his support among Baathist military men based on his own personal part in a failed assassination attempt in 1959. The attempt on a rival leader was botched, with assassins firing from both sides of the street at a car that held the intended victim, actually wounding each other and missing the target. Hussein escaped with his life, fleeing first to Syria and then to Egypt. In Egypt, he briefly attended law school and kept up his contacts with Baathists both in the Iraqi refugee community and back home.

IRAQ AND NEIGHBORING COUNTRIES, 2003

When the Baath Party took power in Iraq in 1963, Hussein returned to Iraq and worked to set up security and intelligence agencies for the Baathist regime. Relying on his intelligence organizations as well as his extensive family connections, he became a major power behind the nominal head of government by 1968. When he took full power in 1979, one of his first steps was a meeting on July 22 of about 1,000 top-level Baath Party members. At least 21 former high-ranking party members were accused of disloyalty and engaging in a plot against Hussein. As each name was read, the individual was taken from the room. Others, fearing their names would be read, tried to demonstrate their loyalty by shouting for

Baath Party

BAATH IS THE ARABIC WORD FOR "REBIRTH." A POLITI-
cal party under that name had originated in Syria in the 1940s. Baath
ideology spread from Syria to other parts of the Middle East, although
Baath-controlled governments emerged only in Syria and in Iraq. The
ideology of the party was based on a mix of ideas: Arab unity, or pan-
Arabism; some limited socialism; and tight control of the economy, as in
the fascist states of Europe, such as Benito Mussolini's Italy. For Iraq, the
idea of pan-Arabism would provide political glue to bind together the
diverse peoples of the nation: Muslim and non-Muslim Arabs, and both
Sunni and Shiite Muslims.

During the cold war between the Soviet Union and its allies on one
side and the United States and its allies on the other that lasted from
1947 to 1991, Baathism seemed to many outsiders to represent a sort of
radical and popular alternative to both communism and to Muslim fundamentalism. By standing above the divisions among Muslims, Baathism
seemed well suited to avoid some of the intense conflict between different religious groups by emphasizing Arabic ethnic identity. On the other
hand, the ideas and methods of the Baathists were a far cry from the
democratic ideals of the United States and the countries of Western
Europe.

Baathism, as a pan-Arab ideology, worked to bring together some of
the diverse population of Iraq. However, the Kurds in the northern
region of the country spoke their own non-Arabic language and were
not ethnic Arabs. Although many were Sunni Muslims, Kurds as a group
sought their own national independence and rankled under the control
of the Arab-dominated regime run by the Baath Party out of Baghdad.
Other divisions in the nation were also hard to pacify or reconcile, as
Shiites in the south resented Sunni dominance from Baghdad, and
everywhere in the country, the most intense loyalties were very local in
nature: to family, to the clan, or to the specific tribe.

Indeed, although Baathism nominally called for unity of all Arabs, it
was mostly Hussein's close family members and fellow Sunnis, especially
from his hometown of Tikrit, who held the choice positions within his
regime. Other Arabs, particularly Shiite Muslims, generally were not
admitted to the inner circle. As in fascist regimes, the economy was run
by a combination of state-operated enterprises and closely controlled
private companies. Religious and ethnic opponents were ruthlessly suppressed, much resembling the Nazi regime of Adolf Hitler in the 1930s
and 1940s.

the death of those removed. Over the next few days, the accused party members were executed. To be sure of the loyalty of his new associates, he had them participate in the execution, and reportedly some of the dead bodies had hundreds of bullet holes. The deputy prime minister, who had been in Syria on business, was seized at the airport and shot dead without trial.

The Kurds' goal of an independent homeland was probably the most severe challenge to national unity faced by the Hussein regime. Even before he had emerged as formal head of state, Hussein ordered two Kurdish towns leveled to the ground in 1974. The Iraqi air force fiercely attacked Kurdish towns, burning out the Kurdish civilian communities. An estimated 1.5 million Kurds became refugees in the early 1970s, and Iraqi troops pushed some 100,000 Kurds out of the country into Iran. More than once, Iraqi soldiers shot Kurdish resistance fighters as they attempted to surrender. Tens of thousands of Kurds were forcibly resettled into the desert of southwestern Iraq.

Stories leaked out of the country that Hussein personally shot cabinet officials or military officers who dared to disagree with him. Hussein did not deny the stories, and whether they were true, they contributed to the loyalty out of fear that many of his associates felt. Of course, such ruthless power has a tendency to enforce itself, as those seeking to stay in the regime offer unwavering support and report any disloyalty among others. Ordinary citizens who spoke out against the regime were denounced by witnesses, arrested, and tortured. Wives and daughters of protesters were put in special cells where they were methodically and repeatedly raped. Sometimes the home of a dissident was bulldozed to the ground. When a prisoner died under torture, his or her body would be returned to the family with a bill for the coffin and funeral. Insult or criticism of Hussein or the Baath Party was a crime punishable by life imprisonment or execution.

Even under this brutality, in some ways Iraq moved into the modern era. The Baath regimes improved education, raised the status of women, and brought drinking water and electricity to previously primitive regions of the country. Unlike some of the neighboring countries, Iraq was ruled by secular, or nonreligious, leaders, and adherence to Muslim rules of daily life was far more lax. Women were allowed to wear makeup, dress in Western clothes, pursue professional careers, and drive their own automobiles, quite distinct from the status of women in nearby Saudi Arabia, Afghanistan, or Iran. With improved education, Iraqis with engineering and business degrees operated modern industries, oil refineries,

This portrait of Saddam Hussein and his family included his daughters and sons, as well as their spouses. Son-in-law General Hussein Kamel (second from right in rear) was later executed on orders from Saddam Hussein for his 1995 temporary defection and revelation of weapons programs. *(Reuters/Landov)*

television and radio stations, banks, trucking companies, shipping facilities, and a large bureaucracy. Baghdad grew into a modern, thriving city, with superhighways, high-rise office buildings, first-class hotels, apartment houses, and a population of more than 4.5 million people.

Hussein's personal lifestyle was lavish, with millions of dollars spent annually on building and maintaining opulent palaces. His sons were notorious for their extensive automobile and art collections—and personal misbehavior. A cult of personality surrounded Hussein, with workers mounting huge wall murals, statues, and photos of Hussein in every public space. The tried-and-true methods of dictators—building loyalty through constant propaganda—seemed to work. Although exiles from the country grumbled that Hussein's regime was a brutal dictatorship, it was hard to find any voices of dissent inside the country, probably out of a mix of real loyalty and fear of punishment for criticism.

In 1980, Hussein began the eight-year war with Iran, in which hundreds of thousands of soldiers and civilians on each side were killed. Iraq spent an estimated $80 billion on weapons, with the war consuming a large part, sometimes as much as 30 percent, of the country's total budget. The weapons came from France, China, and the Soviet Union. Britain imposed an embargo on arms sales to Iraq, but even so, British companies sold equipment, such as uniforms and other defense-related goods to Iraq. Furthermore, both Britain and the United States helped Hussein build up his local arms industry with technical support and equipment, and by encouraging other nations to supply weapons to Iraq. The United States regarded a victory by Iraq as preferable to one by Iran, and although the United States was officially neutral, American policies in the 1980s showed a definite pro-Iraqi leaning.

The Soviet Union sold SS-1 Scud missiles to Iraq, a type of surface-to-surface missiles with a 150- to 190-mile range. The Iraqis reworked the missiles, reputedly increasing the range of some to more than 500 miles. The Scuds were very inaccurate, as they could only be aimed in the general direction of an enemy location or town, often landing a mile or more away from the target point. However, the modified Scuds, launched from western Iraq, could easily reach Israel, and the Israelis feared Hussein planned to use the Scuds to attack them with poison gas, biological weapons, or with radiological or nuclear weapons. Although the Soviets eventually stopped supplying parts for the Scuds, Iraq continued to get repair parts from other sources, including North Korea.

The Soviet-built SS-1 missile, known as the Scud, was transported, raised, and launched aboard a special vehicle, making it hard to track down and destroy. *(DOD Defense Information Center, March ARB, California)*

The Iraqis developed an impressive arsenal of conventional weapons, that is, weapons suited to the battlefield rather than mass attacks on civilian centers. For example, the Iraqis had hundreds of advanced howitzers (cannons) that fired 155-millimeter shells, some with a range of 25 miles, manufactured in Austria and South Africa. Armored, self-propelled six-wheeled artillery pieces made in Iraq could travel 55 miles an hour on a paved road and could fire a heavy shell with a range of 23 to 34 miles. Before the invasion of Kuwait in 1990, the Iraqis had more than 3,000 artillery pieces, more than 4,000 tanks, and some 2,800 armored personnel carriers.

In addition to conventional weapons, Hussein had an ambitious program to build weapons of mass destruction, or WMDs. During the war with Iran, Hussein developed factories for the production of poisonous gas and the missiles and artillery shells to deliver the gas. Later evidence showed that the country had a serious program to build nuclear weapons. Using information publicly available in the United States, Iraqi scientists and technicians built machinery for uranium isotope separation, a necessary step to provide the fuel for nuclear warheads. In 1981, Israeli aircraft conducted a lightning raid to bomb the Iraqi Osiraq nuclear reactor near Baghdad in an attempt to prevent the Iraqi development of a nuclear weapon. After the Osiraq raid, Iraq rebuilt its program, and it was going strong by the late 1980s. Although the Iraqis abandoned the program after Operation Desert Storm (as the Persian Gulf War was called) and under close weapons inspection, observers regarded the idea of a nuclear-armed Hussein as especially frightening.

After Iraq and Iran ended their war in 1988, Hussein's army reputedly numbered more than 500,000 troops. Although some were ill trained and poorly equipped, at least 100,000 had sophisticated weapons and were members of the elite Republican Guard divisions that were disciplined and quite loyal to the regime.

After the many expenses of the long war with Iran, Hussein's regime was strapped for money. Although revenue from oil sales continued to come into the country, oil prices were subject to the decisions of the international Organization of Petroleum Exporting Countries (OPEC). In 1989–90, OPEC allowed oil production to increase and oil prices to drop. As a consequence, Iraq found it difficult to make payments on its huge $70 billion war debt, much of it owed to neighboring Kuwait and Saudi Arabia. Furthermore, Iraq complained that some of the other members of OPEC exceeded their allowed oil quotas. Hussein especially

Oil Revenue

EVER SINCE THE EARLY 1970S, THE INTERNATIONAL price of oil has been loosely controlled by the Organization of Petroleum Exporting Countries (OPEC), with its headquarters in Vienna, Austria. At OPEC meetings (usually twice a year), the oil ministers of some 13 countries from the Middle East, South America, Asia, and Africa gather to set production limits, or quotas. By limiting the supply of crude oil each country produces, the organization can drive up the price of oil. However, each member country has an incentive to cheat on the quotas, that is, to produce more than they promised in order to get a somewhat higher share of the sales. For this reason, OPEC is not always effective as a cartel. Of the approximately 1,000 billion barrels of oil presumed to be in reserves underground, about 10 percent or 100 billion barrels, are located in Iraq. Saudi Arabia holds about one quarter, or 260 billion barrels, of the world reserves; and Kuwait has another 95 billion barrels. The smaller Persian Gulf States have about 105 billion barrels of reserves.

When Hussein ordered the invasion of Kuwait and threatened Saudi Arabia and the smaller gulf states, observers feared that he was on the way to controlling more than half of the world's oil reserves and, as a consequence, the world's supply and price of oil. Since so much of the economies of Europe, the United States, and Japan depends on oil products such as gasoline and heating oil, Hussein's invasion was seen as extremely dangerous not just to Kuwait, but to the world economy.

complained about Kuwait and the United Arab Emirates as flooding the market with cheap oil, as the price fell from more than $21 to approximately $15 per barrel. Iraq exported about a billion barrels a year, so each barrel's fall in price meant the loss of billions of dollars per year in Iraqi oil revenue.

Hussein claimed he had other special grievances against neighboring Kuwait. He asserted that Kuwait had stolen more than $2.4 billion in oil from the Rumaila oil field that straddled the border between Iraq and Kuwait, and he argued that the Kuwaitis were still drawing oil from the Iraqi side, sometimes by drilling the oil wells on a diagonal under the border. Hussein demanded that Kuwait forgive or write off the some of the $10 billion war debt owed by Iraq to Kuwait. He argued that Iraqis

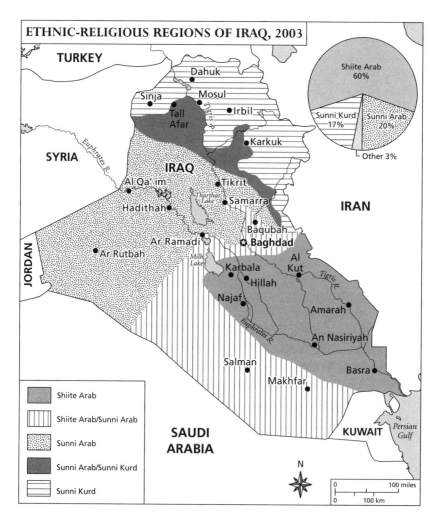

ETHNIC-RELIGIOUS REGIONS OF IRAQ, 2003

Shiite Arab 60%

Sunni Kurd 17%

Sunni Arab 20%

Other 3%

Legend:
- Shiite Arab
- Shiite Arab/Sunni Arab
- Sunni Arab
- Sunni Arab/Sunni Kurd
- Sunni Kurd

had been fighting for the Arab cause against the Iranians, and that as a fellow Arab State, Kuwait should convert the loan to straight foreign aid for the military effort. He made other demands on the Kuwaitis, including ceding lands on the Persian Gulf that would give Iraq more access to the open sea. Hussein also brought up the fact that Kuwait was governed during the days of the Ottoman Empire out of the city of Basra in southern Iraq. The British division after World War I, he claimed, was artificial and arbitrary, and Kuwait should have been designated a province of Iraq when the mandates were set up.

As causes to go to war, all such arguments were pretty flimsy, and most of the world assumed that when Hussein raised these points, he was simply trying to intimidate Kuwait into forgiving the war debt and possibly making some concessions to lease lands on the gulf. Despite the fact that he had overwhelming military strength, diplomats assumed he could get what he wanted by threats, rather than by invasion. So, when Iraqi troops rolled over the border into Kuwait in August 1990, the world was stunned.

4

THE PERSIAN GULF
WAR OF 1991

—◆─◦◦◦◦──────────────────────────────

The Persian Gulf War of 1991 had a very clear casus belli, the Latin term still used to refer to the "cause of war." On August 2, 1990, Hussein ordered his army to move across the border with Kuwait and invade it. The invasion came as a shock to the world. Since the formation of the United Nations in 1945, no sovereign nation that was a member of the United Nations had ever invaded another sovereign UN-member nation. The largest wars in which the United States had participated since World War II had been the Korean War (1950–53) and the Vietnam War (1964–75). In both those wars, the combatant countries were not UN members, and both wars were caused by communist forces fighting to reunite a nation that had been divided by recent diplomatic agreements.

Almost all UN members regarded the invasion of Kuwait by Iraq as a clear-cut violation of the principles of the United Nations respecting the sovereignty of nations. It was seen as an outright, unjustified attack by one nation on another. The 15-member Security Council of the United Nations passed immediate resolutions calling on Iraq to withdraw, threatening the use of force if Iraq did not comply. Between August 1990 and January 1991, the United States and other nations began to assemble military forces in neighboring Saudi Arabia, both to protect that country from an invasion by Iraq and to show the Iraqi government that if military force was required to remove Iraqi presence from Kuwait, it would be available. Operation Desert Shield, which consisted of moving U.S. troops into Saudi Arabia for the needed buildup, began within days of the Iraqi invasion of Kuwait.

In the United States, President George H. W. Bush aligned political support in Congress, and polls showed a high degree of public support for demanding that Hussein remove his troops from Kuwait. Meanwhile, stories of Iraqi atrocities against the Kuwaitis leaked out, both from escaping refugees and from witnesses inside Kuwait who sent out faxes and made phone calls describing the brutality of the Iraqi troops. Confirmed stories of rape, looting, and murder of innocent civilians shocked the world.

For all of these reasons, by mid-January 1991, there was a clear set of justifications for using military force against Iraq. Those justifications ranged from reasons based in international law to more practical and emotional reasons derived from the situation on the ground. Iraq controlled huge oil reserves and by seizing Kuwait, had suddenly acquired more oil resources. With Iraqi troops able to move on into Saudi Arabia if not opposed, Hussein would be in a position to control more than half of the world's oil resources if he so chose. The brutality of his regime toward Iraqis who opposed his rule was well known as were his criminal treatment of prisoners of war and the atrocities of his troops against the Kuwaiti civilian population.

When the United States began the air phase of Operation Desert Storm, as the actual war was called, in mid-January 1991 after the failure of Hussein to respond to UN resolutions, the die was cast. The war was seen not only in the United States but throughout Europe and even in much of the Muslim and Arab world as a fully justified response to an act of aggression by the Iraqi dictator. Only rarely in world history had there been such a degree of international consensus on the justification for war.

Because of the wide international support, President Bush and his advisers, particularly Secretary of State James Baker and Secretary of Defense Richard Cheney, were able to line up financial and military support from many nations. Although the figures varied as the Coalition was assembled, by the time of Operation Desert Storm, there were 34 nations in the Coalition. While some, such as Spain and Portugal, contributed only small naval units, and others, such as Poland and the Czechoslovakia, contributed just a few specialized troops, other Coalition members made major contributions. Quite notable was the participation of Egypt, Syria, Qatar, Bahrain, and Saudi Arabia. These Arabic-speaking Muslim countries, like the European allies, were convinced that Hussein had acted completely outside the law and had to be stopped.

President George H. W. Bush, who served 1989–93, worked hard to line up domestic and international support to oppose the Iraqi takeover of Kuwait in 1990. *(Library of Congress)*

Saudi Arabia, Britain, and France contributed not only ground forces but also aircraft and pilots, so when U.S. general Norman Schwarzkopf launched the first air attack on the night of January 16–17, and then a month later the ground attack on February 24, he was in charge of a truly international force of about 575,000 troops. U.S. units made up most of the strength, but the international character of the Coalition reflected the fact that the opposition to Hussein's aggression was not simply an American idea. Rather, the Coalition showed that Hussein had offended the world, and the world was aligned to stop his outlaw behavior.

Operation Desert Storm itself was divided into two phases. With Iraqi troops and heavy armor, including hundreds of Russian-built tanks, dug into defensive positions, Schwarzkopf and his military advisers conducted an extensive bombing campaign that represented the first phase. Within 30 days, Coalition missiles and bombs had destroyed some 1,300 Iraqi tanks, 1,100 artillery pieces, and 850 armored personnel carriers. Among the first targets were command and control centers, that is, buildings and

camps that contained the leadership of the Iraqi forces and their communication equipment. Another early set of targets was all air-defense and
fighter aircraft. Hussein had ordered about 140 of his military aircraft to
fly out of the country to take refuge in Iran; however, 56 other aircraft were
destroyed on the ground, and 42 in the air. The Coalition aircraft also
attacked dozens of Iraqi anti-aircraft missile ground sites.

Still other targets included Scud missile sites. The so-called Scud was
an Iraqi-modified Soviet surface-to-surface (SS) missile, with a range of
several hundred miles. Despite the efforts to destroy these missiles before
they could be launched, Hussein's forces lobbed a total of 40 of them on
the nation of Israel. The apparent reason for this action was to provoke
Israel into retaliation. Had Israel done so, it would have put the Arab
nations in the Coalition in a difficult position, because they would have

found themselves fighting a fellow Muslim Arabic nation in an alliance with the Jewish state of Israel. No doubt some Arab countries would have withdrawn from the Coalition in those conditions. However, the United States prevailed on the Israelis not to retaliate, and one by one, Coalition forces tracked down and destroyed most of the Iraqi Scud launchers. Other Scuds were launched toward Saudi Arabia, and one caused the largest single group of casualties when it detonated over a barracks housing U.S. troops there. Twenty-eight Americans were killed in that single missile attack on February 25.

As the bombing and missile attack on Iraq continued, many other important targets were selected for destruction, including telephone exchanges, electric power plants, highways and bridges, and other facilities of the infrastructure of the country. Although care was usually taken to make sure the weapons hit the specific target so as to restrict the number of civilian casualties, hundreds of innocent civilians died in these attacks. Even with laser-guided or television-camera-guided missiles, the amount of collateral damage, the term used for unintended civilian deaths and injuries, was tragic. Of course, when civilians were killed or wounded from such attacks, Hussein's information officials would arrange visits to the site for foreign journalists. He hoped that repeated pictures of such tragedies would weaken the political will in the United States and among the populations of the other Coalition nations.

The second phase of Operation Desert Storm, the ground phase of the Persian Gulf War, lasted just over four days, almost exactly 100 hours. There were several reasons that the war moved so rapidly. One was that a month of air bombardment partially had destroyed many of the Iraqi military units and their equipment. Another reason was that the bombardment had had a demoralizing effect on surviving Iraqi soldiers, and they were willing to surrender when Coalition troops appeared. Thousands of the Iraqi soldiers did not feel much loyalty to the regime, and some happily surrendered rather than risk their lives for a system they did not support. In fact, so many Iraqis surrendered in the first 24 hours of the ground war that the Coalition officers stopped counting when the number passed 30,000.

Other reasons for the rapid victory included a brilliant maneuver by the Coalition troops. Instead of attacking into Kuwait to expel the Iraqi forces, Schwarzkopf ordered a wide-swinging invasion by American units through the Iraqi desert to the west of Kuwait. Meanwhile, Arab units drove directly toward Kuwait City. The wide swing out to the west,

Collateral Damage

IN THE SANITIZED JARGON OF WARFARE, THE TERM *collateral damage* refers to the destruction of unintended civilian structures and the killing or injuring of innocent people when an intended military target is being attacked. By contrast to the firebomb raids over London, Berlin, Coventry, Dresden, and Tokyo in World War II, the Coalition's weapons in the both the Persian Gulf War of 1991 and the Iraq War in 2003 were especially chosen to limit collateral damage rather than to increase it.

In Iraq, U.S. and British forces carefully selected targets of military significance and worked to avoid hitting civilian facilities, especially mosques, schools, and hospitals. Knowing that U.S. and British forces sought to limit such collateral damage, the Iraqi military based their troops and weapons storage facilities in civilian residential neighborhoods. Even so, the fact that the British and Americans used guided munitions, which could follow a laser beam directly to a specific target, reduced the number of civilian casualties.

Television cameras in Baghdad recorded nighttime bombing raids that often lit the sky with spectacular detonations and fires, broadcast simultaneously by media around the world. Most of these attacks, even in crowded Baghdad, were aimed at specific government buildings, presidential palaces, and military facilities. Whenever there were civilian casualties, whether from American or British bombs or from falling Iraqi anti-aircraft missiles, the Iraqi regime accused its attackers and attempted to win political sympathy for its cause through television and other news coverage of the tragedy. Because of this, limiting collateral damage was not only humane policy; it helped mitigate international criticism.

in a grand side movement that brought heavy forces against the flank of the Iraqi troops rather than directly to their front, worked well. As Iraqi officers and troops began to realize that they were being cut off from the west and encircled, they began a headlong retreat northward, hoping to pull back toward the center of Iraq and the capital, Baghdad.

As convoys of Iraqi military vehicles and stolen civilian cars and trucks filled with Iraqi soldiers fled from Kuwait City northward, U.S. aircraft attacked them, leaving a trail of destroyed vehicles and spilled loot across the desert north of the city. The press dubbed the wreckage

Hail Mary Maneuver

DURING THE PERSIAN GULF WAR, GENERAL NORMAN Schwarzkopf organized a surprise attack that circled far out into the Iraqi Desert to the west of Kuwait. In order to move the troops and equipment into position before the attack, high security was maintained. When they moved forward in an encircling movement to cut off the retreat of Iraqi troops from Kuwait, he dubbed the tactic as the "Hail Mary maneuver." This name comes from a football strategy in which a pass is thrown far downfield in hopes that a receiver will be there to catch it. In turn, that name comes from the Catholic prayer directed to Mary, the mother of Jesus, as a plea for her aid. The press repeated Schwarzkopf's use of the term for this attack on the left flank of the Iraqi army, and it immediately caught the public's fancy.

the "Highway of Death," although later investigation showed that most of the targeted troops simply ran off into the desert, leaving the vehicles and scattered stolen goods behind to be destroyed from the air.

Perhaps the simplest reason why the war was over so quickly was that the objective was very limited. Schwarzkopf was under orders to evict the Iraqis from Kuwait. When it appeared that all the Iraqi troops were rushing through the Iraqi desert toward home, he arranged for surrender. Later, editorial writers and commentators wondered why Schwarzkopf had ordered a halt to the advance, and why he had not "gone on to Baghdad." The reasons were simple and straightforward. He had no justification for that action, and his orders were specific: to liberate Kuwait. It was obvious both to the Coalition military commanders and the political leadership in Washington, D.C., and in Europe that the liberation of Kuwait was justified by Hussein's actions but that the United Nations, the U.S. Congress, and the other members of the Coalition had not endorsed a Coalition invasion of Iraq. In particular, the Muslim and Arab members of the Coalition were unprepared to support any military action that would have the purpose of overthrowing Hussein's regime.

The aftermath of the short war stretched out over the next decade, and in that aftermath were some of the causes of the Iraq War of 2003.

At the surrender table, the Iraqis agreed that they would refrain from using airplanes over both northern and southern Iraq. They were however allowed to use helicopters in these two "no-fly zones." The zones would be patrolled by British and U.S. aircraft to enforce the rules and to keep all Iraqi fighters and bombers from the regions. Encouraged by this agreement, minorities in both the south and the north of Iraq hoped to overthrow Hussein's control.

Within Iraq, the Shiite Arabs living in southern Iraq near Kuwait and the Iranian border believed that with the collapse of the Iraqi army, they could overthrow the oppressive government domination of their region. However, when Coalition troops did not come to their aid over the month following the end of the war, the Iraqis used both ground forces and helicopters to ruthlessly suppress a southern Shiite uprising. Thousands of Shiite Muslim leaders were arrested, and hundreds were executed without trial.

General Norman Schwarzkopf and Lieutenant General Khalid, commander of the Joint Forces in Saudi Arabia, meet with Iraqi officers in Safwan, Iraq, March 31, 1991, to set the terms of the Iraqi surrender in the Persian Gulf War. *(DOD Defense Information Center, March ARB, California)*

In the northern provinces of Iraq, Kurdish rebels also hoped to be able to eliminate the brutal and ruthless Iraqi control of that region. Again, rebels were pursued by Iraqi troops, and many Kurdish refugees fled into neighboring Turkey. Turkey, concerned that its own Kurdish population might challenge Turkish authority, turned back the refugees. Under the protection of the no-fly zone rules, however, local Kurdish regimes established a loose form of local control within Iraq over the next few years with little interference from Hussein's army. A small contingent of international troops helped provide a haven for the Kurds.

The United Nations insisted that the Iraqi regime admit weapons inspectors to ensure that Iraq eliminated its WMDs. Until Iraq complied with its surrender agreement to destroy those weapons, the UN would ask its members to impose economic sanctions on the regime. That meant that trade to Iraq by other nations would be severely limited. As the inspectors began their work, they were surprised to learn that Iraqi scientists had come very close to building an atomic bomb.

5
SEPTEMBER 11, AFGHANISTAN, AND IRAQ

A t about 8:45 A.M. (EST) on September 11, 2001, a commercial airplane crashed into one of the twin towers of the World Trade Center in New York City; a little more than 15 minutes later, a second plane struck the other tower. At about 9:40 A.M., another plane crashed into

The September 11, 2001, attack on the twin towers in Manhattan that killed nearly 2,800 people shocked the nation and the world. *(Library of Congress, Prints and Photographs Division [LC-DIG-ppmsca-02137])*

On September 11, 2001, terrorists crashed an American Airlines passenger plane into the west face of the Pentagon, causing extensive damage to the building and dozens of casualties. *(Tech. Sergeant Cedric H. Rudisill, Department of Defense)*

the Pentagon in Washington, D.C.; a fourth airplane crashed about 80 miles southeast of Pittsburgh, Pennsylvania, around 10 A.M. Almost 2,800 people died in the World Trade Center tower fires and collapse, with another 200 dying at the Pentagon and in the Pennsylvania crash.

In the immediate aftermath and shock of the terrorist attacks of September 11, 2001, it was not clear what organization lay behind the planning of the airplane hijackings and the destruction they had caused. However, as information was quickly gathered about the hijackers, it became publicly known they were associated with the organization known as al-Qaeda (also al-Qa'ida).

In Arabic *al-Qaeda* means "the base" or "the foundation" in the sense of an underlying framework, such as the chassis of an automobile. The organization by that name grew out of a relief agency established in Afghanistan by a member of a wealthy Saudi Arabian family, Osama bin Laden. Bin Laden had provided funding and aid to the families of anti-Soviet guerrillas killed there.

President George W. Bush, who had taken office in January, ordered that the assets of organizations linked to al-Qaeda be frozen. He also ordered a military campaign to track down and destroy the organization where it was based in Afghanistan. Operation Enduring Freedom, as the U.S. government officially named it, began October 7, 2001, with early combat operations including a mix of air strikes from ground- and sea-based aircraft, as well as Tomahawk cruise missiles launched from both British and U.S. ships and submarines. As the attacks began, critics pointed out that Afghanistan had been extremely difficult to conquer in the past,

After the September 11, 2001, terrorist attacks, al-Qaeda leader Osama bin Laden went into hiding. This image from a videotape, showing bin Laden at left, was released by the U.S. Department of Defense. *(Department of Defense)*

with the British giving up the effort in the 19th century and the Soviet Union withdrawing after an eight-year war that had begun in 1979. The objectives of the Operation Enduring Freedom were to destroy the terrorist training camps, to capture al-Qaeda leaders, and to stop terrorist activities in Afghanistan. At first, the United States gave the Islamic fundamentalist Taliban regime in Afghanistan an opportunity to arrest and turn over al-Qaeda leaders, but as the Taliban refused to do so, the overthrow of that regime became another objective of the operation.

The term *Taliban* referred to the former students from religious schools in Pakistan, committed to a radical version of fundamentalist Islamic beliefs. In 1993, the "students" had established a government in Afghanistan that imposed strict adherence to a code of conduct that included the elimination of all education for girls and women and the prohibition of women appearing in public unless they were covered from head to toe. The decrees of the Taliban were enforced with public beatings and executions.

Despite fears to the contrary, Operation Enduring Freedom was a quick success in a military sense. Among the reasons was a strong American-led international force allowing for massive air strikes and the commitment of ground troops. When the British government joined in the military operation under their own Operation Veritas on October 16, the British explicitly included as an objective the destruction of the Taliban regime. In addition to the British, some 68 nations offered support, with a total of 27 participating with military forces. Local Afghan groups long opposed to the Taliban, many organized in the Northern Alliance, played a major part in overthrowing the regime. It is estimated that when Operation Enduring Freedom began on October 7, the Taliban controlled 80 percent of Afghanistan, but within two months, the Taliban government was defeated, leaving only pockets and remnants of forces behind.

By October 20, the missile and bomb attacks had destroyed nearly all of the Taliban air defenses. Special forces teams linked up with anti-Taliban leaders and coordinated attacks. On November 9, the city of

Mazar-e Sharif was liberated from the Taliban, and over the next few days, Taliqan was also freed from its grip. Kabul, the capital, was liberated on November 13 and Jalalabad on November 14. These victories were owing to a combination effort of Northern Alliance troops and international special forces units. The defection of numerous military units previously committed to the Taliban also sped the victory. U.S. Marines moved in on November 25, establishing the Rhino airstrip and an operating base south of Qandahar.

The last Taliban stronghold, Qandahar, fell to Northern Alliance troops on December 7, and marines took the Qandahar airport on December 13. By that time, groups of Taliban and al-Qaeda forces had retreated to mountainous hideouts, mostly on the Pakistan border in the region of Tora Bora and Zawar Kili.

The number of American troops killed in military engagements during Enduring Freedom was 10, with another three killed in friendly-fire accidents. Other types of accidents brought the total death toll to 38. Never before in history had the United States led the conquest of another country as large as Afghanistan with so few casualties to U.S. troops.

While regular U.S. troops sought to track down and arrest leaders of al-Qaeda and the Taliban, an interim government under Hamid Karzai was established. On January 3, an international force of 4,500 troops, under the command of British general John McColl began to assist in the stabilization of Kabul. Marines at Qandahar were relieved by U.S. Army troops of the 101st Airborne Division. Meanwhile, Coalition forces including troops from Australia, Canada, Denmark, France, Germany, and Norway cooperated in Operation Anaconda to round up remnants of al-Qaeda and Taliban forces. The European nations contributed their troops and support as part of a decision by the North Atlantic Treaty Organization (NATO), which for the first time, invoked a mutual-defense treaty clause. In this case, the al-Qaeda attack on the United States was regarded by the NATO members as equivalent to an attack on each member country, and NATO agreed to the goals of Operation Enduring Freedom.

France provided combat fighter aircraft that flew from a base in the former Soviet republic of Kyrgyzstan on fighter and reconnaissance missions. The French aircraft were later relieved by a group of Danish, Dutch, and Norwegian fighters and a refueling tanker aircraft. Italy approved the deployment of 2,700 soldiers to the effort, while Germany approved up to 3,900 soldiers.

SEPTEMBER 11, AFGHANISTAN, AND IRAQ

In May 2002, an international force of 400 soldiers from the U.S. Army, Canadian army, and Afghan military forces operated in the Tora Bora region of Afghanistan, gathering intelligence and denying the Taliban and al-Qaeda access to underground sites. This Chinook CH-47 helicopter is preparing to pick up waiting troops. *(Staff Sergeant Jeremy T. Lock, Department of Defense)*

Many nations provided logistical or transport help to Operation Enduring Freedom. For example, both the Ukraine and Romania provided transit rights for aircraft to fly over these countries to Afghanistan. The former Soviet Union republics of Uzbekistan and Kyrgyzstan provided airfields. A Bulgarian airport on the Black Sea became a staging area for U.S. equipment. The gulf states of Oman and Bahrain also allowed the use of bases on their territory.

In addition to the ships deployed by the United States and Britain, Canada sent the frigate *Halifax* to the area and committed five other ships and 1,900 soldiers to the effort. In what the Canadians called Operation Athena, their forces, headed by General Peter Devlin, included groups from the 2nd Mechanized Brigade Group, a battalion group from the Royal Canadian Regiment, and other smaller contingents. On October 2, 2003, two Canadian soldiers in Afghanistan were killed and five wounded when their jeep hit a land mine.

As al-Qaeda and Taliban leaders and officers were captured, many were singled out for further interrogation. On January 10, 2002, the first shipment of such detainees was sent to a temporary camp at the U.S. naval base in Guantánamo, Cuba, known as Camp X-Ray (so-called out of military habit to assigning a name to each letter of the alphabet, this camp being *X*).

Although many al-Qaeda and Taliban leaders were captured, bin Laden and some of his closest associates escaped, apparently across the loosely guarded border into the northwest frontier region of Pakistan. In this part of Pakistan, control is in the hands of local tribal authorities; the Pakistan army and security forces normally do not venture into the region. There, al-Qaeda organization leaders could therefore stay put or move on without being detected or caught, to major cities in Pakistan or other refuges around the world. Critics of Operation Enduring Freedom pointed out that while Afghanistan no longer represented an al-Qaeda stronghold, the central objective of tracking down and arresting the group behind the 9/11 attack had not fully succeeded. Supporters, on the other hand, claimed that the military operation had put al-Qaeda on the defensive and showed the terrorists that the United States would not accept such acts of war without severe, immediate, and crushing retaliation. In the future, any government would think carefully of the consequences before allowing al-Qaeda to operate openly within its borders.

The fact that the terrorist organization was not a national government had meant, however, that it was extremely difficult to use military force against it. The military forces of nations such as the United States, Britain, Canada, France, and Italy, especially when supported by local forces, could quickly overwhelm a nation such as Afghanistan. However, in the new world of asymmetrical warfare—that is, where one of the opposing forces is apt to be smaller but more flexible and elusive—such military forces were only partially successful in conducting the necessary mix of intelligence and police work required to track down and capture particular individuals or groups of terrorists.

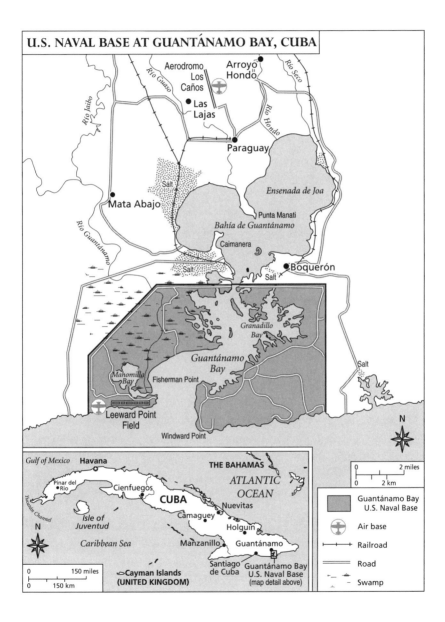

U.S. Base at Guantánamo Bay

AFTER THE UNITED STATES HELPED CUBA GAIN ITS independence from Spain in 1898, the settlement included the agreement that the United States could maintain several military bases on the island. Only one was ever established, surrounded by chain-link fences and completely independent of any Cuban governing power. It is a naval base located on Guantánamo Bay, on the southeastern coast of Cuba. Even after Fidel Castro led a revolution there in 1959 and Cuba became a Communist country, Castro continued to recognize the treaty obligation that allowed the base at Guantánamo. The base was a convenient place to hold prisoners from the point of view of the U.S. military, because only military law could apply there, not civilian court jurisdiction. Camp X-Ray, and later Camp Delta, allowed the government to hold and interrogate prisoners captured in Afghanistan during Operation Enduring Freedom, and these prisoners could not appeal to U.S. courts for release.

Camp Delta at Guantánamo Bay in Cuba, successor to Camp X-Ray, serves as a detention facility for the interrogation of enemy combatants captured in Afghanistan. *(Staff Sergeant Stephen Lewald, Department of Defense)*

SEPTEMBER 11, AFGHANISTAN, AND IRAQ

Two months after the success in Afghanistan, U.S. president Bush surprised allies and enemies alike with a statement in his State of the Union speech, on January 29, 2002. He alluded to an "axis of evil" consisting of states that supported terror. He named Iraq, Iran, and North Korea as part of this axis. The speech stirred controversy both abroad and in the United States. Although NATO had willingly supported the United States in the operation in Afghanistan, the assertion that these three major countries were on notice from the United States seemed inappropriate to many observers. For one thing, the three countries apparently had little in common. North Korea was geographically isolated from the other two and was run by a repressive Communist regime. Iran was governed by a fundamentalist Islamic regime, while Iraq was dominated by the brutal secular, or non-religious, dictatorship of Saddam Hussein under the Baathist one-party system. Furthermore, none of the three countries had any known record of having supported al-Qaeda.

Through the rest of 2002, as the United States and Great Britain began to attempt to build arguments and support for a preemptive military action against Iraq (an attack before Iraq could take action), these

U.S. secretary of defense Donald Rumsfeld (left) with Hamid Karzai, president of the interim government of Afghanistan, at a joint news conference in February 2003 *(Helene C. Stikkel, Department of Defense)*

issues and others became widely debated. Although a connection between the Afghan government and al-Qaeda had been clear, there was very little evidence of any connection between al-Qaeda and Hussein's regime in Iraq. Nevertheless, President Bush and Prime Minister Blair began to make a case for a preemptive strike against Iraq. Editorialists, commentators, and politicians loudly debated the issue of preemption, or prior action, and the justification for such an attack in this instance.

Over the months between January and October 2002, the United States used its influence at the United Nations to attempt to get that organization to enforce its numerous resolutions against the regime of Saddam Hussein. The story of how the United Nations tried to ensure that Iraq had no weapons of mass destruction was a series of setbacks and frustrations.

6

WEAPONS INSPECTIONS

Between the end of the Persian Gulf War in 1991 and December 1998, the United Nations attempted to ensure that Iraq had fully disposed of all its weapons of mass destruction (WMDs) and the capabilities to make those weapons. WMDs included chemical weapons, such as poison gas and biological weapons that would carry diseases such as anthrax. Nuclear weapons such as the atomic bombs the United States used against Japan at the end of World War II were also a type of WMD, as were radiological weapons, or "dirty bombs," that consisted of a high-explosive weapon that dispersed radioactive material over a wide area. All such weapons could cause "mass destruction" because a single weapon could kill thousands or even hundreds of thousands of people, with one detonation.

Part of the reason why the United States and Great Britain decided to launch Operation Iraqi Freedom in March 2003 was because after the Persian Gulf War, Iraq did not live up to its surrender agreements. After the 1991 war, Iraq agreed to allow UN inspectors to come to Iraq to verify that the country had disposed of any and all WMDs; however, inspectors who went to Iraq in 1991 soon found that the Hussein government continued to try to hide chemical, biological, and nuclear weapons programs. As this issue became a major controversy before and after the Iraq War of 2003, it is important to know the facts of the early rounds of arms inspections.

The idea of inspection to verify conformity with an arms agreement had developed at the end of the cold war between the United States and the Soviet Union. Under the arms agreements between the United States and the Soviet Union, each side agreed to allow the other's military teams to visit. These teams would look at missile sites, military airfields, weapons storage areas, missile silos and missile launchers, and weapons production facilities. As each side destroyed weapons under the agreements, the other side's inspectors would witness the destruction or sometimes even throw the switch that would dynamite a site's facilities.

In the United States, a special agency was created in 1989 to provide the experts who would do the inspections and verifications of the Soviet sites, known as the On-Site Inspection Agency (OSIA). OSIA sent numerous teams to Russia, the Ukraine, and other countries such as Romania and Poland to verify the destruction of weapons and missiles. At the same time, the Soviet Union sent similar teams to the United States. The inspection system worked because both sides had agreed to cut back their nuclear weapons and weapons-delivery systems. That meant that each side would honestly and openly reduce the number of missiles, submarines, and aircraft under the treaties that marked the end of the cold war.

Applying that same idea, the United Nations hoped to be able to verify the cooperation of Iraq in destroying its WMDs by sending international teams who would visit Iraqi sites and confirm that Iraq was destroying the weapons. Between 1991 and 1998, a UN agency called the United Nations Special Commission (UNSCOM), conducted the inspections, along with representatives of the International Atomic Energy Agency (IAEA). The system would work to confirm and verify destruction, but only if Iraq cooperated as the United States and the Soviet Union had cooperated. In fact, given the experience of OSIA in arranging such inspections, the UNSCOM and IAEA teams relied on OSIA to provide experts, staff, translators, and contractors to help with their mission.

However, although Iraq claimed to accept the inspectors and to cooperate, the Iraqi government attempted to prevent the inspection teams from actually finding or seeing its weapons program. The inspection teams, without cooperation, tried to track down and locate the existing weapons. Since the inspectors were not armed and could not use force, it was quite easy for the Iraqis to prevent the inspectors from gaining access to specific buildings, factories, airfields, storage areas, or other sites that the inspectors believed contained weapons. The same method that had worked well between cooperating countries such as the United States and the Soviet Union simply could not be applied to a

WEAPONS INSPECTIONS

Following the Persian Gulf War in 1991, teams from the United Nations Special Commission (UNSCOM) visited Iraq to inspect and to try to ensure the elimination of weapons of mass destruction. Here, an UNSCOM team examines artillery shells designed to deliver deadly mustard gas. *(UN/DPI Photo)*

country that refused to cooperate. Over a seven-year period, the extent of the failure and the frustration of the inspectors mounted.

UNSCOM made numerous discoveries and encountered stiff resistance from the Iraqi government over the years 1991–98, despite the Iraqi claims to be cooperating. After a four-year gap, in late 2002, a second round of inspectors were sent, in a new group: the United Nations Monitoring, Verification and Inspection Commission, or UNMOVIC. UNMOVIC worked for nearly four months but discovered no WMDs.

The story of the obstacles encountered by both UNSCOM and UNMOVIC helps explain why many governments around the world refused to trust or believe the Iraqi representatives when they denied they had WMDs. Over and over, the UN Security Council passed resolutions condemning the failure of the Iraqis to cooperate and sometimes threatening the use of force to obtain further compliance. The first of the resolutions was passed immediately after the end of the Persian Gulf War, on April 2, 1991. Resolution #687 required Iraq to unconditionally accept the destruction, removal, or "rendering harmless" of all WMDs, all ballistic missiles with a range of more than 150 kilometers (about 93 miles), and all the facilities for making WMDs or missiles. The resolution provided for the system of ongoing monitoring and verification. Three days after the Security Council passed the resolution Iraq officially accepted it. In accord with the resolution, Iraq then provided an "initial declaration" describing chemical weapons and some missiles. The declaration denied the existence of any Iraqi biological or nuclear weapons. The initial agreement of Iraq to cooperate with Resolution #687 could be considered part of the Iraqi surrender agreement at the end of the Persian Gulf War.

In June 1991, the inspections began. Within two weeks, inspectors began to run into trouble. UNSCOM personnel backed up by experts from the IAEA tried to intercept Iraqi trucks carrying calutrons, large electromagnetic machines used to separate two isotopes of uranium in order to refine out the fissionable uranium-235 that can be used to fuel atomic bombs. The Iraqis fired weapons at the inspectors' vehicles as they tried to intercept the calutrons. Later, the equipment was located and destroyed under international supervision. This episode was only the first of many cases of armed resistance to the inspectors, and it was one of the early cases that proved the Iraqis lied about their WMD programs.

In response to this delay tactic, the Security Council passed another resolution demanding cooperation. In fact, over the period of 1991–98, the Security Council passed a total of 12 resolutions. Later, the record of those repeated resolutions helped show that an inspection-verification approach to the WMD question in Iraq without the backup of force was very hard to implement.

These 12 resolutions condemning actions by Iraq and demanding further cooperation had little effect. Often Iraqi officials would threaten the UNSCOM inspectors, warning that they might be shot or their aircraft fired at. When inspectors asked for access to locations that contained archives related to weapons programs, they were sometimes simply denied access. In 1993, when the Iraqis prohibited UNSCOM inspectors from using their own aircraft, the United States, France, and Great Britain bombed anti-aircraft sites in southern Iraq. Only after the bombing raid did Iraq allow UNSCOM to resume using its own aircraft. Through 1993 and 1994, large amounts of chemical weapons, together with production equipment, were located and destroyed. To further test the UN, in October 1994, Iraq sent troops to the Kuwait border and then withdrew them only when threatened with force.

UN Resolutions Regarding Weapons of Mass Destruction in Iraq, 1991–1998

Date	Resolution Number	Content
April 3, 1991	687	Demands that Iraq accept inspection and destruction of WMDs
August 15, 1991	707	Demands disclosure of proscribed weapons and programs
October 11, 1991	715	Demands that Iraq accept all UNSCOM personnel
October 15, 1994	949	Demands that Iraq cooperate fully
March 27, 1996	1051	Approves monitoring of imports to Iraq; requires cooperation
June 12, 1996	1060	Finds Iraq in clear violation of UN resolutions
June 21, 1997	1115	Condemns Iraq's actions; demands access to sites
October 23, 1997	1134	Demands cooperation; warns of additional sanctions
November 12, 1997	1137	Condemns Iraq for violations; imposes travel restrictions on Iraqis
March 2, 1998	1154	Endorses an understanding in which Iraq has already agreed to cooperate
September 9, 1998	1194	Condemns Iraq for suspending cooperation
November 5, 1998	1205	Demands that Iraq rescind decisions not to cooperate

When General Hussein Kamel, the minister of industry and former director of Iraq's Military Industrialization Corporation fled Iraq for Jordan on August 7, 1995, he revealed details regarding the prohibited weapons program and the concealment program under way. The son-in-law of

Saddam Hussein, Kamel brought out of Iraq his younger brother, also married to a daughter of Saddam Hussein, and their families, apparently fearful of the internal fights in the Hussein family. In addition, Kamel brought with him several crates of documents showing details of the WMD programs in Iraq, which he gave to UNSCOM.

In the light of this information, further documents were uncovered in Iraq. Finally, in late 1995, Iraq admitted that it had a biological weapons program but denied that the material had been "weaponized" (loaded into bombs or artillery shells). Later, Iraq reversed this position, submitting a new report that admitted biological weapons had been weaponized. A large cache of documents hidden on a chicken farm revealed previously denied programs of VX nerve gas production and nuclear weapons development. Kamel was lured back to Iraq with promises that all would be forgiven. After crossing the border, he was taken into custody and shot, on February 23, 1996, according to rumors, on the direct orders of Uday Hussein, his brother-in-law and Saddam Hussein's elder son.

Although the exact details of what Kamel told the UN inspectors were kept quiet for years, it was revealed in 2003 that he had ordered the destruction of Iraq's chemical WMDs and he had told UNSCOM that he believed they had all been destroyed. He had also claimed that while the WMDs had been destroyed, Iraqi scientists had taken blueprints, plans, and technical drawings to their homes so that the Iraqis could start up a new WMD program once the inspectors left.

In March 1996, Iraq denied UNSCOM access to specific sites for up to 17 hours. In 1997, Iraq complained that American personnel working for UNSCOM were serving as spies to the United States and expelled the American staff members. In response, the United Nations withdrew all the inspectors until the standoff was resolved by Russian negotiation. This account of problems does not include many episodes of denial of access, threats to personnel, holding of UNSCOM personnel under armed guard for periods of up to several days, and sequences of denial, agreement to cooperate, then refusal to cooperate.

By 1998, the UN group had come to realize that the inspection system simply did not work. After further Iraqi interference with the inspection, the UN inspectors pulled out in December. Then in mid-December, U.S. president Bill Clinton ordered a series of air raids over Iraq in Operation Desert Fox aimed at military installations in retaliation for the Iraqi noncompliance. Some suspected WMD sites were bombed out; however, the UN inspectors did not return.

After the UNSCOM inspectors withdrew from Iraq because Hussein had denied them access to many sites, U.S. president Bill Clinton ordered a series of air raids on Iraq in Operation Desert Fox, in December 1998. Among other sites hit was the Baghdad headquarters of the Baath Party, with arrows showing damage points. *(Department of Defense)*

On November 27, 2002, under a new UN Security Council resolution, #1441, a team of arms inspectors under UNMOVIC went to Iraq to initiate yet another round of inspections. Again, the inspectors encountered the same pattern of evasion, although on this round, the UNMOVIC inspectors did not try to conduct surprise inspections. All of the sites they went to had been cleared out well in advance. The United States did not participate in the UNMOVIC teams. By March 2003, the UNMOVIC inspectors had not discovered any major evidence of continuing WMD programs. However, when UNMOVIC staff presented Iraqis with questions about what had happened to known quantities of weapons that had been identified by earlier UNSCOM teams, the Iraqis had no answer and no documents. In this regard, UNMOVIC inspectors reported that they had been unable to verify the destruction of the WMDs.

Meanwhile U.S. and British intelligence agencies, working from intercepted radio and telephone messages, satellite reconnaissance and

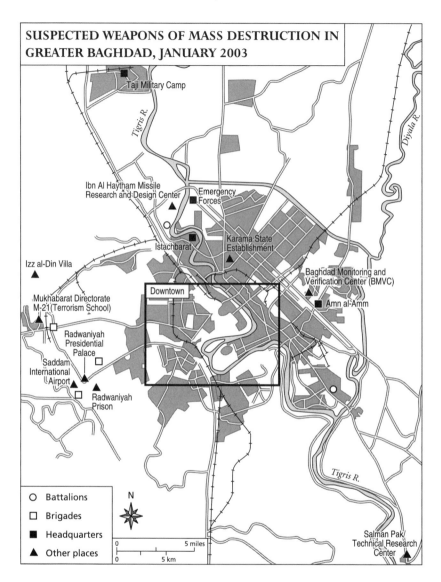

SUSPECTED WEAPONS OF MASS DESTRUCTION IN
GREATER BAGHDAD, JANUARY 2003

aerial photos taken from aircraft over-flights, and other sources, remained convinced that the Iraq regime continued to conceal WMD programs. Both British prime minister Blair and U.S. president Bush presented evidence derived from intelligence sources to their respective legislative bodies and publics that Iraq held WMDs and had concealed them in violation of UN resolutions. As the two leaders sought support in the United Nations for a new resolution that would provide an ultimatum to the Iraqis, they presented their intelligence findings to the press and to the United Nations.

The prior 13 resolutions had demanded cooperation and threatened the use of force in the face of noncompliance. The Iraqi pattern of claiming to cooperate while actually refusing to cooperate had not however led the UN to retaliate thus far with anything more than a few air raids and economic sanctions that limited trade with Iraq. Even so, most of the members of the UN Security Council were not convinced that further Iraqi refusal to cooperate would justify an all-out attack on Iraq. President Bush and Prime Minister Blair set out to convince the other member nations to join them in putting an end to the Iraqi evasion and to their possible weapons programs with an ultimatum followed by the use of armed force if needed.

7
UN DEBATES AND
RELUCTANT FRIENDS

The decision-making body at the United Nations that decides on possible military action against member states is the Security Council. When the Allies at the end of World War II established the United Nations, they arranged that the Security Council would include five permanent member nations. The five were the major Allies against Nazi Germany and imperial Japan in that war: Great Britain, the United States, France, China, and the Soviet Union. With the breakup of the Soviet Union in 1991, Russia took over the permanent seat of the Soviet Union at the UN Security Council. Each of these five nations holds a veto power, which means that even if all the other permanent members vote in favor of a motion, a single vote against a motion from a permanent member stops the resolution from passing. In addition to the five permanent members, representatives from another 10 countries sit on the council. These 10 serve for two-year terms. These nonpermanent members can vote, but none can veto a measure.

In early 2003, the UN Security Council consisted of representatives of these 15 nations:

Permanent members (5): China, France, Great Britain, Russia, and the United States

Term ending in December 2003 (5): Bulgaria, Cameroon, Guinea, Mexico, and Syria

Term ending in December 2004 (5): Angola, Chile, Germany, Pakistan, and Spain

UN DEBATES AND RELUCTANT FRIENDS

The General Assembly of the United Nations held a moment of silence on its opening day, September 10, 2002, in memory of the terrorist attacks on the United States the year before. *(UN/DPI Photo by Mark Garten)*

How these nations might vote on the use of force against Iraq became a major topic in the news in early 2003. If the right resolution could be written, observers then believed that the United States and Britain could count on a positive vote from certain nations. The United States had alliances and friendly relations with many of the nonpermanent members. If China and Russia would agree not to vote at all (that is, to abstain), such a measure might pass with a majority vote. France had already announced that it would oppose such a resolution and would veto it. Advocates of war claimed that a simple majority vote, even with a French veto, would give a kind of UN approval for war.

From late January through early March, secretive talks went forward, with frequent leaks to the press about possible types of resolutions. Soon, the positions of several countries became clear. A very strong resolution against Iraq would receive support from only three or four countries: Britain, the United States, Spain, and probably Bulgaria. France and Russia

Jus ad bellum
THE JUSTIFICATION FOR WAR

WRITING IN THE 13TH CENTURY, THE ROMAN CATHOLIC philosopher Thomas Aquinas enunciated the principles of what constituted a just war. Because he wrote in Latin, the language used by the Catholic clergy at that time, his terminology has survived to this day: *jus ad bellum,* "justification for war." Later authorities added three more concerns to Thomas Aquinas's as part of the modern analysis of whether a war is justified.

1. The war should be declared on proper authority.
2. The war should have a proper cause, or casus belli.
3. There should be a reasonable chance of success.
4. The act of war should be in proportion with the offense of the nation being attacked.
5. War should only be used as a last resort.
6. The real reason for the war should be a right intention and should be the stated reason.
7. The outcome of the war will lead to a more just result than if no war had occurred.

Those in Europe and America who opposed the idea of a war against Iraq argued that on every count the war was not justified, whereas those who advocated the use of force against Iraq believed strongly that on every count the evidence showed that a war would be justified, especially if Iraq were given one last chance by the United Nations to cooperate fully and to reveal its WMD programs, and if it failed to do so. The latter group argued that under such a circumstance, all seven *jus ad bellum* reasons would have been met.

were opposed to such a resolution, and France consistently threatened to use the veto. Even countries such as Mexico and Chile that had friendly and close relations with the United States could not support a war resolution. Germany also opposed a strong resolution against Iraq.

The reason for the debate and the severe division over the issue was a classic one that had to do with justifications for war. People argued differently on how the principles that would justify a war might or might not apply in this case. The arguments ran through the Security Council and world public opinion. In most of Europe and in other countries, the majority of people opposed a war because they saw it as not justified.

Despite disagreements on whether a war with Iraq would be a just war, opponents and advocates of action against Iraq could agree on certain things. Hussein had ruled under an extremely cruel and repressive regime and had used torture against his own people. Before 1989, Hussein had ordered the use of WMDs in the war against Iran, resulting in an estimated 100,000 casualties, and in Halabja against Kurds in 1988, resulting in an estimated 5,000 deaths and 10,000 injuries to civilians. Altogether the extermination campaign in 1988 against Kurds took about 100,000 lives. Then in 1990, Iraq had without justification attacked Kuwait and had been forcibly ejected only when the UN endorsed the use of force to free that country in 1991. Those were the facts of history.

However, what had happened since 1991? The facts from that period were hard to uncover and agree upon. Although Iraq had had WMD programs in the early 1990s, the world knew that Iraq had ended some of those programs. On the other hand, it was also clear that Iraq had evaded inspection and put obstacles in the way of inspectors as if it were hiding more WMDs. Furthermore, intelligence information suggested but did not prove that Iraq still had such weapons and ways to make them.

When Prime Minister Blair presented his report, informally called the "Blair Dossier" to the British Parliament in September 2002, he stressed all of the evidence that his intelligence agencies had collected that suggested Iraq still maintained WMDs. Blair also detailed the numerous atrocities of the Hussein regime against the Iraqi people, including the gruesome tortures and executions without trial. Without stating the parallel explicitly, Blair reminded Parliament and the British people of the situation facing Europe in the 1930s when Adolf Hitler had defied the will of the League of Nations and imposed a ruthless regime in Germany. "We know," he said, "from our history that diplomacy, not backed by the threat of force, has never worked with dictators and never will work. . . . The threat is not imagined. The history of Saddam and WMD is not American or British propaganda. The history and the present threat are real." In Britain, however, not everyone, including some members of Blair's own Labour Party, were as sure.

The official UN group conducting inspections and verification of the Iraqi claim, UNMOVIC, was first constituted in early 2002, and began its inspections in November 2002. Hans Blix headed the UNMOVIC team. Although both the British and Americans claimed they had found

Just War or Not?

WORLD OPINION DIVIDED SEVERELY OVER THE JUSTICE of a war against Iraq. On each of the seven "just war" counts, opponents and proponents of war disagreed on interpretation of the facts. This would be a classic yes-and-no analysis of each point.

1. The war should be declared on proper authority.

   Opponents: Only a new vote by the Security Council would grant proper authority.
   Proponents: Iraq had disobeyed prior Security Council resolutions that threatened force if disobeyed, and Resolution #1441, passed in 2002, gave sufficient authority.

2. The war should have a proper cause, or casus belli.

   Opponents: There was no clear evidence of WMDs, according to chief UN inspector Hans Blix.
   Proponents: There was no clear evidence that Iraq had eliminated its known WMDs, according to Blix.

3. There should be a reasonable chance of success.

   Opponents: The casualty rate in a war might be so high that success would not be clear.
   Proponents: The Iraqi regime was weaker than it had been in 1991, and few troops would be needed to defeat the Iraqis.

evidence that Iraq continued with its WMD programs, the team headed by Blix did not find evidence of any active program in Iraq. However, Blix did report finding some missiles that were capable of flight beyond the 150-kilometer (93-mile) range, and his team found factory equipment for making rocket motors for more such missiles. Blix also said the Iraqis still did not cooperate fully in providing information about destruction of older weapons, but the UNMOVIC teams encountered less difficulties in carrying out inspections than the UNSCOM teams had. Both the British and the U.S. intelligence services provided the

4. The act of war should be in proportion with the offense of the nation being attacked.

Opponents: Obstruction of inspections is not an act of war.
Proponents: The regime was dangerous, had WMDs, and was a threat to security unless removed.

5. War should only be used as a last resort.

Opponents: Inspections should continue before war is the only option.
Proponents: Saddam Hussein had used up his chances to cooperate.

6. The real reason for the war should show right intent and should be the stated reason.

Opponents: Prime Minister Tony Blair and President George W. Bush really wanted access to Iraqi oil or had other motives.
Proponents: Possession of WMDs by a ruthless, terror-sponsoring state is the real and sufficient reason.

7. The outcome of the war will lead to a more just result than if no war had occurred.

Opponents: Thousands of civilian and military casualties could be avoided.
Proponents: If the war is conducted quickly and humanely, the result will be freedom for the Iraqi people and the elimination of threat to the region.

UNMOVIC teams with information, and Blix sent teams to investigate their evidence that the Iraqis were still hiding WMDs, moving them about the country, or operating hidden factories. In every case, his teams found no continuing weapons program.

Blix was walking a diplomatic tightrope. He had to be careful to state exactly what UNMOVIC found and no more or no less. If he exaggerated the resistance he found with the Iraqis, his report might convince the UN Security Council to endorse a war against Iraq as a just war. On the other hand, if he glossed over the Iraqi resistance and made it appear

A new inspection effort was mounted by the United Nations under the direction of Hans Blix. Here, Blix, executive chairman of the UN Monitoring, Verification, and Inspection Commission (UNMOVIC), speaks briefly to the press after reporting to the Security Council in November 2002. *(UN/DPI Photo)*

they were more cooperative than they really were, he could be setting up the United Nations for another round of obstruction tactics of the Iraqi regime. War or peace could hang on how he phrased his report.

Debates on these issues continued not just among the delegates to the UN Security Council, but around the world. In Germany, France, and Britain, hundreds of thousands of demonstrators in the streets loudly protested against any war vote by their governments. Smaller demonstrations on both sides of the issue in the United States revealed the split in opinion in America. However, American public opinion polls, depending on exactly how the questions were phrased, tended to show between 65 percent and 75 percent favoring a final ultimatum to Hussein and military action. If other nations were assumed to be in support of the American position, the vote in favor of war was even higher.

For Americans, another issue was also important. If the United States attacked Iraq after a brief warning, it would be a preemptive strike, in this context, preventing Iraq from taking military action first. Some commentators identified a new Bush "preemptive war" doctrine. They saw this doctrine as a dangerous and unethical step for a nation as powerful as the United States. However, the traditional American policy of only reacting, not going first, the president argued, no longer applied in a world with WMDs and with states that sponsored terror.

In an effort to convince the wavering members of the Security Council that the U.S. and British position was correct, Secretary of State Colin Powell made a presentation of evidence from classified sources to a meeting of council members on February 5, 2003. Television stations broadcast the meeting live. Within the U.S. cabinet, Powell was reputed to be the one who argued for a cautious and peaceful approach to the Iraqi

Preemptive War—A New American Doctrine?

IN 2002 AND EARLY 2003, BOTH U.S. PRESIDENT GEORGE W. Bush and British prime minister Tony Blair argued that in the new world of terrorist activities, it was necessary to take military action *before* a potential enemy took the first step. The terrorist attacks on September 11, 2001, had killed almost 3,000 people. Poison gas attacks or nuclear weapons could kill 10 or 100 times as many people with one detonation. The regimes in Iraq, Iran, and North Korea were known to have programs to build such weapons. The three countries, to various degrees, had also in the past supported terrorists. Did this mean that they should be given an ultimatum to give up their weapons of mass destruction or face an unprovoked military attack?

The United States had only rarely attacked another country without the other nation taking the first overt act of war. In World War I, German submarines had sunk American ships before President Woodrow Wilson asked for a declaration of war. In World War II, the United States did not participate until the Japanese attacked Pearl Harbor in the Hawaiian Islands. In the Vietnam War, the United States pointed to the firing on U.S. destroyers in the Gulf of Tonkin as a case of the enemy taking the first action. Exceptions included a quick attack ordered by President Ronald Reagan on the island of Grenada in 1983 before any overt act by that small country. However, if the United States tried to preempt Iraq from supporting terrorists with weapons of mass destruction by an armed attack on that country, it would represent a departure from the main American historical precedent of going to war only in response to an overt act by the enemy.

On February 5, 2003, U.S. secretary of state Colin Powell presents evidence showing Iraq has not complied with UN demands to eliminate weapons of mass destruction. *(UN/DPI Photo by Mark Garten)*

issue. Observers believed that having him make the presentation at the United Nations might be convincing to the other nations' representatives.

Powell presented material drawn from satellite photography, from intercepted telephone conversations, and from other sources. Some of the material indicated that the Iraqis were making continued efforts to conceal chemical warfare manufacturing and weapons from the inspectors. Evidence that chemical plants were installed on trucks for moving over the highways all were suggestive that the Iraqis still had WMD programs. However, the evidence presented by Secretary Powell did not appear to change many minds. Representatives of the various members of the Security Council responded, politely thanking Powell for his presentation. It was clear that only Britain, the United States, and Spain still favored action; France, Russia, China, Germany, and most smaller countries remained unconvinced. After a few more weeks of trying to line up a majority in the Security Council, Britain and the United States abandoned the effort. No vote was taken.

Meanwhile, the United States attempted to get the 16-member NATO to offer support to fellow member Turkey in preparation for a possible war. NATO, made up of most western European nations, as well as Canada and the United States, had supported Operation Enduring Freedom in Afghanistan and might be convinced to support a war against Iraq. In the NATO forum, France and Germany both opposed such an action, which would need to be taken unanimously. Several smaller countries in the NATO alliance agreed with the U.S. and British position. However, on the whole, NATO refused to endorse the action or to aid Turkey in preparation for war.

As a last negotiation effort to line up support, the United States attempted to get Turkey to agree to join in the coalition supporting an attack on Iraq, or at least, to provide unimpeded passage across Turkey for U.S. troops. Discussions with Turkey proceeded for several weeks, often focusing on the amount of financial aid the United States was prepared to offer Turkey in the event of war. To many cynical commentators, the fact that Turkey's participation seemed to depend on whether the United States would offer $24 billion or $29 billion in aid appeared almost corrupt.

President Bush announced that the United States might lead an invasion of Iraq with a "coalition of the willing." Cynics punned that he was seeking a "coalition of the billing." In the end, the United States and

Members of the UN Security Council listen intently as Secretary Powell presents satellite images, intercepted phone calls, and other intelligence information regarding Iraqi WMD programs. *(UN/DPI Photo by Mark Garten)*

IRAQ WAR

On March 16, 2003, British prime minister Tony Blair (left) meets with U.S. president George W. Bush in the Azores Islands, working with the prime ministers of Spain and Portugal in an attempt to find a diplomatic solution to the Iraqi refusal to cooperate with the UN. *(Larry Downing, Reuters/Landov)*

Turkey could not agree on terms of Turkish participation. In fact, another issue divided the United States and Turkey. That was the role that Turkey would play in an occupation of northern Iraq. The Kurds in that region supported the United States and Britain against the Hussein regime; however, the Kurds vowed that they would fight any effort of the Turkish army to occupy their lands. Rather than face such a war-within-a-war between potential allies, it was simpler for the United States to abandon any effort to line up Turkish support.

By mid-March 2003, it was clear that the United States and Britain, together with a few smaller nations, were willing to take on the challenge of ending the Hussein regime. The U.S. and British governments, despite the clear reluctance of either the United Nations or NATO to provide support, were ready to issue their own ultimatum to the Hussein regime.

This ultimatum was issued on March 17. President Bush ordered the first missiles to strike Iraq on March 19, 2003, marking the beginning of the war.

8

AMERICANS AT WAR

Week 1

Despite the fact that the United Nations had not endorsed the position of the United States and Britain, those two countries proceeded to act and to refer to their action as that of a coalition. The term suggested much wider participation, similar to that in the Persian Gulf War of 1991. Supporters of the U.S. administration pointed out that other coalitions and single nations had engaged in military actions not endorsed by the UN Security Council. During the administration of President Bill Clinton, for example, the United States had conducted air strikes in 1998 against the Serbian government to drive them from the province of Kosovo, without any UN sanction. The French government had also intervened in several countries in Africa, including the Ivory Coast and Chad, without even approaching the UN Security Council for an endorsement.

The Coalition in 2003, however, had participation only from the United States (with some 145,000 military personnel in Iraq during the peak of the fighting) and Great Britain (some 41,000 likewise), with smaller contingents of troops from Australia (2,050), Poland (200), and the Czech Republic and Slovakia (400). By contrast, in 1991 during the Persian Gulf War, France, Egypt, Syria, and Saudi Arabia all contributed large numbers of forces, and a total of more than 30 nations provided some form of military assistance.

Although the government of Canada had taken a strong stand against participating in the war in Iraq, readers of Canadian newspapers were surprised to learn that some 31 Canadian soldiers and an unidentified

The massive ordnance air blast (MOAB) is known informally among U.S. troops as the "Mother of All Bombs." Precision-guided and weighing more than 10 tons, it is the largest nonnuclear conventional weapon in existence and was a key part of the "shock and awe" campaign over Baghdad in March 2003. *(Department of Defense)*

number of Canadian airmen were fighting alongside the British and U.S. troops in Iraq. Although not sent as members of a single, Canadian-officered unit, these servicepeople were "seconded" (given a secondary assignment) as part of interservice training and duties to either British or U.S. units that were deployed to Iraq. Originally stationed in Europe, when the units were moved to Iraq, the seconded Canadian troops simply went with them as part of the units. In addition, several Canadian airmen served aboard AWAC aircraft that served to coordinate military operations over Iraq. Since opposition to the war was very vocal in Canada, especially in Quebec, such information led to criticism of Prime Minister Jean Chrétien.

Although the U.S. Defense Department suggested that there would be a campaign of "shock and awe," the air strikes during the first days of the war were not the sort of terror bombing, or "blitz," of the general city that the term seemed to imply. Rather, all the munitions dropped from aircraft or fired as missiles from ships in the Persian Gulf were precision-guided; that is, every weapon was aimed at a specific strategic target, such as a military base, a radar or artillery installation, or a specific government office building. By contrast, in the 1991 Persian Gulf War, only some 10 percent of the munitions dropped on Iraq were precision-guided. The consequence was that in 2003 there were relatively few incidents of collateral damage, or deaths or injury to civilians who were not connected with the Iraqi regime.

The language of the war spread rapidly, as journalists who traveled with the military units, the so-called embedded reporters and photographers, relayed news from the front line back to newspapers and television. In addition, press briefings in Qatar, as well as interviews with Defense Department personnel in Washington, soon added to the public's growing vocabulary of military terms. As many as 1,500 sorties, or individual air missions, were being flown each day. Pilots were given assigned targets but also sought out and struck at emerging targets and targets of opportunity, that is, military units or equipment that they chanced to spot on the ground. They had to be extremely careful not to become confused in the "fog of war"—the oft-cited allusion to the confusion on a battlefield—and destroy a Coalition tank or unit on the

This FA-18C Hornet launches from aboard USS *Kitty Hawk* in support of coalition forces in Iraq. *(Photographer's Mate 3rd Class Todd Frantom, Department of Defense)*

ground. Such accidental attacks or casualties from "friendly fire" still happened. In fact, in one such incident, a U.S. F-16 aircraft fired on an American Patriot anti-aircraft battery on March 23, the fourth day of the war. Fortunately, there were no casualties.

Central Command (CENTCOM), based in Florida, conducted the U.S. military operation, and its commander was General Tommy Franks, who like General Schwarzkopf in the Persian Gulf War, spent much of his time near the front. While Schwarzkopf had been based in

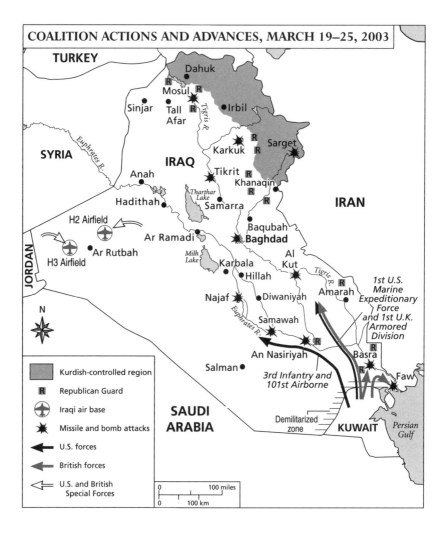

Market Explosions

THE IRAQI GOVERNMENT CLAIMED THAT U.S. BOMBS had caused two explosions in Baghdad on March 26, 2003, that killed a total of 17 civilians. While local witnesses emphatically blamed the Americans for the attack, journalists who visited the sites observed a number of facts that suggested that explosions were due either to a fallen Iraqi anti-aircraft missile or to an intentional detonation set off by the Iraqis to create a propaganda effect. For one thing, the shallow depressions in the ground caused by the explosions were a very small fraction of the deep craters caused by the American missiles that hit buildings and other targets. Witnesses claimed they had heard American aircraft overhead, but the attacking American aircraft tended to fly so high that they were rarely heard. Nevertheless, photographs of the devastation to the two market areas appeared around the world and helped contribute to international opposition to the war.

Saudi Arabia, Franks set up his headquarters in the city of Doha in the small gulf state of Qatar. There, he delegated much of the contact with the press to a young African-American brigadier general, Vincent Brooks.

As relayed through the press, the public not only learned a lot of military jargon in the first week of the war; they soon became more familiar with the geography of Iraq, especially in the region between the Kuwait border and the capital city of Baghdad. One of the first two cities as military objectives inside Iraq was the port of Umm Qasr, where Iraq had its only oil-export terminals for loading crude oil aboard tankers bound for the Persian Gulf and the world markets. About 30 miles further north lay the large city of Basra, largely inhabited by Shiite Muslims presumed to be opposed to the regime of Saddam Hussein. U.S. and British troops would concentrate on capturing the port of Umm Qasr, and the British would focus on capturing Basra. Also close to the Kuwait border were the crucial Rumaila oil fields.

The way to Baghdad, about 260 air miles northwest of Umm Qasr, paralleled the Euphrates River. The invasion would, of course, not go in a straight line but would follow a route closer to 300 miles long, for the most part just to the west of the Euphrates. Along the way were several large cities. The first, about 100 miles into the country, was An Nasiriyah.

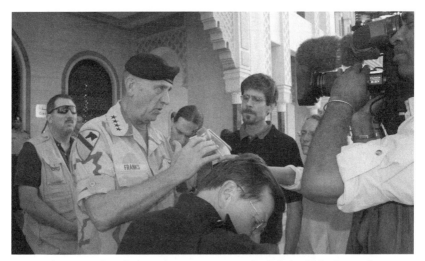

General Tommy Franks, serving as commander of the U.S. Central Command (CENTCOM) gives an impromptu press briefing outside a hotel in Abu Dhabi, in the United Arab Emirates, during a trip to visit troops in the Persian Gulf region. *(Helene C. Stikkel, Department of Defense)*

Another 100 miles or so would lead to An Najaf. Then, almost due north of An Najaf lay the city of Karbala.

The cities of Basra, An Nasiriyah, An Najaf, and Karbala all represented possible resistance points. In addition, Karbala was flanked on the west by the large Ar Razzazah Lake and on the east by the Euphrates River. Even before U.S. forces reached the region, analysts expected a tough fight at the "Karbala Gap," since the freedom to maneuver would be restricted by the two bodies of water to the west and east.

In the first week of the war, from March 20 through March 27, the embedded journalists began to send back reports. Since they were so close to the action, they rarely could comment on the big picture, which could only be obtained from the controlled release of information at the press briefings back at Doha, Qatar. So, for audiences around the world, in the flood of news that came from Iraq, it was difficult to really know how the war was progressing. On the one hand, as units of the 1st Marine Expeditionary Force worked with the British 7th Armoured Brigade to capture the Rumaila oil fields and move on Basra, it appeared at first that Basra would be an early and easy victory. In the same encouraging way, reports that the U.S. 3rd Infantry Division had moved 150 miles into Iraq by the third day of the war, roughly halfway to Baghdad, seemed to suggest that the war would be over quickly.

However, the first days of the war also produced some very disturbing news. Despite claims that Basra had fallen, by the end of the week, units were still engaged in heavy battles in that city. The Iraqi commanding general of the 51st Mechanized Division had surrendered to the British, but units of that division appeared to be still fighting. Then there were some more unexpected developments.

On March 23, 12 soldiers of the U.S. 507th Maintenance Company were reported missing and captured. Among the presumed captured soldiers were two women, Shoshana Johnson and Jessica Lynch. Later investigation of the incident showed that their convoy of vehicles, traveling in the early morning hours, had missed a turn. Several of the trucks ran out of fuel or broke down, delaying them and separating some of the trucks from others. The 507th was not a combat unit but one that was assigned to support a Patriot missile battery, and on the third full day of the war, they were more than 130 miles into Iraq, on the outskirts of An Nasiriyah.

Although later reports on the episode of the 507th Maintenance Company showed numerous mistakes by officers that might have been avoided with better care and training, one of the underlying causes for the capture was simply the rapid advance of the units. Moving large numbers of vehicles day and night required that they "leapfrog" forward, meaning one unit would move ahead 20 to 50 miles, then settle down and refuel armored equipment, Humvees, and trucks, make repairs, and rest. The rest spots, with assigned code names such as "Attack Position Bull" or "Attack Position Lizard," were located by map coordinates and the use of global positioning systems that used signals from satellites to help soldiers find locations in the dark or in the unmarked desert. Meanwhile, another group would catch up with the first, pass it, and then stop several miles ahead at the next planned attack position or rest stop. The leapfrogging tactic had allowed the remarkable advance, halfway to Baghdad within three to four days.

The price paid for the rapid advance was high, however. The tactic involved traveling through unfamiliar territory sometimes with no roads at all or laced with dozens of unmarked roads and intersections. Columns of equipment encountered sporadic resistance and attacks. The movement established no clear front line with the enemy, leaving behind concentrations of Iraqi forces that could harass support columns as they moved to catch up. The rapid advance also meant that fuel would run low if a section of a convoy of trucks was separated from backup fuel tank trucks. The army's formal report of the 507th incident suggested that the problems related to noncontiguous battlefields—that is, the leap-frogging method of advance—reflected the sort of issues the army might face in the future.

Other episodes were also disturbing. Among the Iraqis encountered near Basra were many un-uniformed fighters, wearing civilian clothing with just a few pieces of uniform. As the battles and advancing Coalition columns passed through settled areas, U.S. and British troops had assumed that anyone wearing civilian clothes was a noncombatant. By disguising themselves as civilians, Iraqi soldiers were violating one of the conventions, or rules, of war that protected civilians from being shot.

On March 26, marine Task Force Tarawa reported the capture of a hospital, where, the day before, they took prisoner about 170 Iraqi soldiers who were wearing civilian clothing mixed with military uniforms. At the hospital were stockpiles of weapons and ammunition, as well as about 3,000 chemical suits and gas masks. On the hospital grounds was an abandoned Russian-made T-55 tank. The hospital had been clearly

As U.S. troops advance, they are sometimes greeted as liberators by civilians in the southern region of Iraq. *(Department of Defense)*

U.S. troops sometimes found that the Iraqis had used hospitals and schools as military strongpoints or for stockpiles of weapons. This stash of assault rifles was found along with more than 3,000 chemical-weapons protective suits in a hospital in An Nasiriyah by U.S. Marines on March 25, 2003. *(Captain N. V. Taylor, Department of Defense)*

marked with the Red Crescent, the equivalent of the Red Cross, which meant that it was supposed to be protected from military use and military attack. The use of a hospital as a staging area or supply center for weapons and other military equipment represented another violation of the conventions of war. Under those conventions, attackers would refrain from attacking a hospital or clinic marked with the Red Cross or Red Crescent, assuming it might contain innocent sick or wounded civilians. Some of the Iraqi troops captured belonged to a group known as the Fedayeen Saddam, a dedicated force of irregular fighters who often resorted to terrorist tactics and deceptive measures.

Reports began to filter back of civilians having been "recruited"—under threat of murder of their families, held hostage—to fire on American troops. In more than one episode, a group of Iraqis advanced

Irregular Fighters

PART OF THE DEFENSE THAT THE IRAQIS PUT UP IN THE first weeks of the 2003 war was mounted by irregular troops. By definition, the Iraqi irregulars were often ill-trained men, sometimes recruited from Baath Party groups, who did not wear uniforms and fought in small groups, usually armed only with AK-47 machine guns and rocket-propelled grenades (RPGs). Together with more highly trained and dedicated members of the Fedayeen Saddam, these groups used guerrilla tactics.

This meant that they would not try to defend entrenched positions or lines but would simply fire from cover at the advancing U.S. or British forces, then retreat or drop their weapons to blend into the civilian population. As they advanced, the U.S. Marines would often detain and question all men of military age, no matter how they were dressed, on the suspicion that some were irregular fighters. Although the Iraqi landscape, with its desert regions and irrigated agricultural fields near the rivers, offered little cover for such guerrilla tactics, the cities of Basra, An Nasiriyah, As Samawah, and An Najaf provided cover in the form of alleys, shops, and tightly clustered residences. Because the urban landscape is full of corners, each a natural point of cover and danger, U.S. troops largely bypassed and isolated the cities on their rapid advance. Even so, many of the casualties in the first days of the war came from ambushes and sniper attacks from irregulars.

As these casualties mounted, analysts who predicted a difficult fight ahead for the Americans emphasized the danger posed by irregular

waving a white flag as a sign of surrender, with their hands in the air. When they were among the Coalition troops, the pretense of surrender was dropped, and the group pulled out weapons and opened fire. Other reports trickled out of Basra indicating that one of the reasons the British could not take the center of the city was that civilians were being intimidated into resisting the invasion by the Fedayeen Saddam, which threatened to kill anyone who surrendered to the British. Here and there, Iraqis would welcome the advancing troops as liberators, but for the

forces. On the other hand, the rapid advance toward Baghdad and the rapid defeat of organized regular Iraqi units led others to predict an early end to the war and a quick victory for the Coalition.

U.S. Marines begin to encounter irregular troops, unofficial soldiers dressed as civilians and using guerrilla tactics. Marines detain this man on March 29, 2003, north of An Nasiriyah. *(Oleg Popov, Reuters/Landov)*

most part, the population seemed to be taking a wait-and-see attitude, simply watching without reacting as the tanks, personnel carriers, and trucks passed by on the dusty roads. From time to time, an isolated group of Iraqis would fire on the convoys from a distance, only to disappear back into the general population.

On top of such news, by March 25, a thick sandstorm developed, requiring many of the advancing columns to stop in place and severely limiting the effectiveness of air attacks. At least temporarily, there would

U.S. troops fought under difficult conditions, including having to wear protective gear like this during a blinding sandstorm. *(Staff Sergeant Matthew Hannen, Department of Defense)*

be a lapse in the leapfrog advance. As the sandstorms swept through Iraq and as reports of the bogged-down offensive came through from the embedded reporters, many British and American citizens feared that their sons, daughters, husbands, and wives would be in for an extended and disastrous war.

9

THE HOME FRONT

The television news media began an avid competition for coverage of the war during its first few days in late March 2003. Some channels developed large maps of Iraq that would cover the floor of a studio, then a news anchor would interview an expert on military strategy as they strode over the map. Discussing the engagements, they would point to features such as the Euphrates River, the city of An Nasiriyah, and in the distance, Baghdad, beyond the "Karbala Gap." Each network recruited former military officers to offer commentary on the war.

Some of the retired officers admitted that they were not informed on the day-to-day operation and that their opinions were often only educated guesses. Others expressed shock at the conduct of the war; it seemed to them that numerous mistakes were being made. For example, the Coalition did not take the time to conduct an extended air campaign to soften up the Iraqi forces before launching the ground assault. In the Persian Gulf War of 1991, the air campaign had lasted more than a full month (January 16–February 19, 1991) before General Schwarzkopf had sent in troops. Furthermore, in this attack of 2003, the intent was to defeat the Iraqi armed forces in their own country, which would seem to motivate the Iraqis to fight more vigorously, as they were defending their homeland. In contrast, in 1991, Iraqi morale had collapsed quickly, and many of the tens of thousands of prisoners captured then had indicated that they had little stomach for their invasion of Kuwait. Even so, Schwarzkopf had assembled a massive army of more than 575,000 troops on the ground, composed of many allies, before attempting the very limited objective of expelling the Iraqis from Kuwait. In this war, of 2003, in

Secretary of Defense Donald Rumsfeld

SECRETARY OF DEFENSE DONALD RUMSFELD BECAME the center of several controversies during the first weeks of the Iraq War. As the leading spokesperson for the Defense Department, he was often called upon to explain U.S. policy and strategy at news conferences, sometimes accompanied by the chairman of the Joint Chiefs of Staff, General Richard Myers. Rumsfeld, who had served in Washington in a variety of government positions since the 1970s, had developed a unique manner with the press. Television viewers watching Rumsfeld interact at these press conferences found that they either liked Rumsfeld a lot or were thoroughly annoyed by him. Those who felt positive about him admired his parrying of questions. They chuckled at his ability take a hostile question and spin out an answer that, when studied closely, only stated a commonsense position that the reporter should have known in the first place. Others found those same traits infuriating and evasive.

Secretary Rumsfeld knew that everything he said could and would be used against the administration by some reporters, if possible. For this reason, he scrupulously avoided speaking for the president, for the secretary of state, or for foreign governments. He also carefully avoided giving timetables of predicted success that could be later quoted to indicate a failure to achieve a goal. At the same time, his willingness to undergo heated questioning about U.S. military policies led many to assume that the strategies of employing fewer troops, using the so-called shock and awe bombing strategy, and implementing the method of rapid mobile advance toward Baghdad should be attributed to Rumsfeld and his civil-

which hundreds of miles of Iraqi territory had to be conquered, General Franks was content to operate with many fewer boots on the ground.

As television viewers were often reminded, Iraq was a country "the size of California." Some of the analysts and journalists warned in the first week that the war seemed ill planned and that the Defense Department issued no clear statement of a strategy. A few of the retired generals offering media commentary admitted, however, that a lot of weapons technology and information technology had been perfected in the decade since the Persian Gulf War and that many new tactics had been

ian advisers in the Defense Department. Many in the press corps remained unconvinced when General Myers and Rumsfeld both insisted that the strategies were fully approved by the military leadership.

Secretary of Defense Donald Rumsfeld and the chairman of the Joint Chiefs of Staff, General Richard Myers, insist that the new warfighting strategy is fully supported by the military, despite rumors to the contrary. *(R. D. Ward, Department of Defense)*

developed to take advantage of that technology. Even so, in the first few days of the war, with elements of bad news coming from the embedded reporters and the television analysts, many in the public began to worry that the war would be an extended one.

The practice of placing journalists with the units on the ground was controversial from the first. The Defense Department recognized that the technique of passing information to the press in 1991 had not always worked very well. During the Persian Gulf War, information was given out in press conferences held at the command post in Saudi Arabia, and there was very little reporting from the front. The press only received the information to which the military thought they should have access. Of course, the advantage of that approach, from a military point of view, was that security was not endangered by leaks of important tactical information that could be of use to the enemy.

The downside of the 1991 press conference and news handout approach, however, was that journalists and the public felt that the information was too tightly controlled and that there was no independence of the press. Furthermore, the day-to-day life of soldiers who carried weapons into conflict or who drove the vehicles was simply not visible to the public. Even from the point of view of the military, this was a disadvantage, because the public was not given a chance to see the dedication of the troops on the ground and to identify with their difficulties. If the military wanted the 2003 war to receive public support, it recognized that it had to have a better way of presenting the information than the 1991-style briefing room, with charts and selected camera shots from the air, and the press conference with an officer taking and sometimes evading questions.

The answer in 2003 was the concept of the "embedded" journalist, who was assigned to travel with a specific unit of troops. The embedded reporters knew that the information they relayed from the front line had to be carefully worded so as not to give away specifics regarding position, force level, direction of travel, or anything else that might aid the enemy. On the other hand, they could take pictures and report on dozens of immediate details that reflected the drama, the risk, the day-to-day heroism, and the difficulty of living on the ground without bathing facilities or proper sleeping quarters and of being on the move every day, often under fire. The result gave a sense of immediacy to the reports, although the information was usually so immediate that no clear picture of the gains or of the war as a whole came through. Nevertheless, in terms of public relations, the system worked quite well. Whether the system of embedded reporting represented a victory or defeat for freedom of the press was itself a subject of debate among the press and others.

Retail stores and restaurants reported that business dropped as a large percentage of people stayed home, glued to their television sets, watching the flow of information, reports, filmed stories, analysis, interviews, briefings, and press conferences on any of at least five channels that devoted airtime to nonstop coverage of the war. Some stores, noticing the great decrease in shoppers and sales, went so far as to turn on television monitors to a news channel throughout the shopping area so

THE HOME FRONT

Chris Tomlinson (seated at right) of the Associated Press was a journalist "embedded" with the 7th Infantry Regiment. Here, he eats a "meal ready to eat" at a rest stop about 100 miles south of Baghdad. *(John Moore, AP/Wide World Photos)*

that shoppers could pick up supplies of detergent, paper towels, and other necessities, all the while keeping one eye on Iraq.

The flow of information, opinion, and analysis fed into a sharpened sense of division in the United States. By contrast to World War II and the Persian Gulf War, when the great majority of Americans believed that their country was conducting a just war, the Iraq War immediately seemed to divide opinion. During the conflict, polls tended to show 70 percent or more of the population in the United States in support of the war, depending on how the question was asked. Even so, the minority who felt the war was inappropriate or unjust was extremely vocal.

Close analysis of the news media revealed a growing division there as well. In general, newspapers and television networks that tended to be critical of the policies of President Bush, which included the influential *Washington Post* and *New York Times* newspapers, presented accurate news but with a detectable slant. They tended to present information that highlighted the difficulty of the war, the failure to find any WMDs, and the high and continuing level of criticism of U.S. policies in Europe

Deck of Cards

AT A PRESS CONFERENCE, GENERAL VINCENT BROOKS, the officer who conducted the daily news briefings at U.S. headquarters in Qatar, displayed a deck of 55 cards—modeled on the standard deck of 52 cards—each with the picture and identification of a major wanted Iraqi leader. The cards, he explained, had been distributed to the troops and would be used to try to track down the leaders. The higher-ranking cards of a standard deck were assigned to the highest-ranking and most-wanted individuals. The deck of cards soon became popular among the soldiers in the field and then among civilians in the United States. The deck sold well at convenience stores and newsstands across the country, surprising the card manufacturer and the Department of Defense as well.

The most-wanted leaders of the Iraqi regime were depicted on a deck of cards, distributed to the troops and later sold as a novelty item across the United States. *(Department of Defense)*

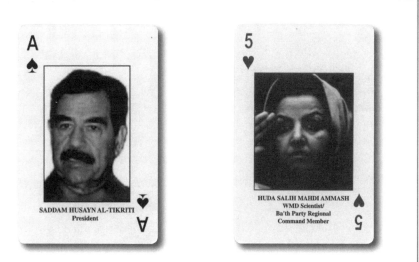

The Ace of Spades, of course, was Saddam Hussein. Among the deck were

Ace of Hearts—Uday Hussein: Hussein's son, chief of the Fedayeen Saddam, head of Iraqi Olympic organization, controlled several media outlets.

Ace of Clubs—Qusay Hussein: Hussein's son, heir apparent to the regime, Baath Party Military Bureau deputy chairman, in charge of intelligence and security.

Ace of Diamonds—Abid Hamid Mahmoud: Personal secretary to Saddam Hussein, in charge of president's bodyguards.

King of Clubs—Izzat Ibrahim al-Douri: Vice chairman of the Revolutionary Command Council.

King of Diamonds—Aziz Salih al-Numan: Baath Party Regional Command chairman.

Queen of Clubs—Kamal Mustafa: Secretary of the Republican Guard and Special Republican Guard.

Ten of Diamonds—Taha Yassin Ramadan: Vice president.

Eight of Spades—Tariq Aziz: Former foreign minister and deputy prime minister.

Five of Hearts—Huda Salih Mahdi Ammash: Weapons scientist, Baath Party Regional Command member, only woman in the deck.

and in the Middle East. On the whole, the Cable News Network (CNN) and the network television channel CBS also tended to focus on that kind of coverage. On the other hand, the MSNBC cable channel and Fox News television channels tended to be far more upbeat and to stress the rapid victories. The differences in treatment were most pronounced in the first week over predictions of eventual outcomes. The so-called liberal media that were critical of U.S. government policy tended to expect the war to last a long time, with many casualties, and to predict disastrous house-to-house street resistance when American troops reached Baghdad. The more conservative newspapers and television channels predicted a rapid collapse of the Iraqi regime.

Even the analysis of public opinion that the news media developed in the early weeks of the war reflected the editorial slant of the particular newspaper or television station. Those with concerns that the war was unjustified emphasized the anxiety felt among the public over the setbacks and negative news. Those who supported the war stressed the very low casualty rates, the rapid advances, and the continuing high rate of support for the president's policies in the polls.

Ever since the end of the Vietnam War in 1975, analysts had noted that the media's ability to bring the war into living rooms of the citizens had reduced the public's acceptance of casualties. Despite all of the efforts to control U.S. casualties in war using improved and more rapid medical treatment of the wounded, better protective gear and body armor, and superior technology and tactics, it was inevitable that there would be some number of deaths and wounded. As the tally of those killed climbed, analysts wondered whether the "Vietnam effect" would take hold. High numbers of casualties, some believed, would lead to weakened support for the war. Others argued that the reason that American public support for the war in Vietnam had declined had less to do with simple casualty rates and more to do with a growing disillusionment with the goals of that war. By contrast, in 2003, a firm majority of the American public appeared to agree that the regime of Saddam Hussein was oppressive, cruel, warlike, and dangerous and tended to believe that the goal of a regime change would lead to the liberation of the Iraqi people. Even so, the debate over whether the regime had possessed WMDs and whether it was appropriate to take measures against the regime without support from the UN Security Council continued into the war itself.

The capture of the U.S. troops in the 507th Maintenance Company, with the media focus on both Private First Class Jessica Lynch and Specialist Shoshana Johnson and their possible fate at the hands of the Iraqis, provided a personalized and dramatic side to the story of confusing troop movements. This fact could be seen in two ways. Opponents of the war argued that driving 300 miles into Iraq in three days exposed the troops to extended supply lines, dangerous possibilities of attacks on their rear, and heightened risk. By contrast, Secretary of State Powell called the lightning speed advance "a heck of an achievement," and much of the public felt the same way.

Analysts wondered what contributed to the quality of sharp division in American opinion. Some attributed it to the way the media had expanded over the decades since the Vietnam War. In the 1960s and 1970s, when only three networks provided television news, and when they all tried to compete for the large middle ground of opinion, no major media outlet could afford to be found on the extremes of opinion. By the 1990s, with the proliferation of television channels due to satellite and cable television, some networks were able to concentrate on winning an audience in a smaller sector of the opinion range. Thus, for example, the new networks, notably Fox News and MSNBC, could afford to be openly critical of the liberal media and could appeal more directly to a conservative audience.

Others claimed that those media outlets dominated by New York and Los Angeles offices were increasingly out of touch with mid-America. In most of the country, the spread of "talk radio," in which members of the public could call in and air their opinions without fear of appearing out of touch, unstylish, or politically incorrect, had led to a forum that gave vent to deeply felt opinions. Those opinions sometimes varied sharply from those held by journalists, intellectuals, and entertainment personalities in the big East and West Coast cities.

Often widely held beliefs were not based on fact. In the wake of the attacks of September 11, 2001, many Americans associated the al-Qaeda terrorists with Saddam Hussein's regime and believed the war on Iraq was a justified response to the attack on America. Although there was no evidence of any substantial relationship between Hussein and al-Qaeda, the public perception that there was such a connection appeared to contribute to a wide undercurrent of support for the administration's decision to invade Iraq.

As in the Persian Gulf War, many people demonstrated their support for the troops by stringing yellow ribbons from trees in public parks and in front of their homes. At the same time, here and there, relatively large

In a show of support for the troops, this woman puts up a yellow ribbon on a tree at the front gate of the naval station in Everett, Washington, in anticipation of the scheduled return home of the aircraft carrier USS *Lincoln* and its 23 support ships. *(Anthony Bolante, Reuters/Landov)*

protest rallies were held against the war. Writers debated every aspect. Was it disrespectful to the men and women in the field to hold demonstrations against the war? Or was it showing the ultimate respect for them to wish that they would be returned safely by calling for an early end to the war? Did the guerrilla tactics employed by the Fedayeen Saddam mean that the Iraqis had begun to violate all the codes of war in a desperate and brutal last gasp? Or were they simply showing their dedication to defend their homeland, just as Americans had done against the British in the American Revolution? After all, it was the American Minutemen in that war who fired from concealed positions and violated what the British then conceived to be appropriate warfare behavior. Did the resort to asymmetrical warfare mean that the Iraqi war machine was almost defeated? Or would it lead to unacceptable levels of U.S. casualties, ultimately proving that the war was a poor idea, poorly executed?

For some, the continuing failure to locate WMDs appeared to be a crucial issue. If such weapons were never found, they argued, it would prove that Bush had entered the war on false pretenses and that the public and Congress had been deceived. Others believed that the WMD question was less crucial than ending a corrupt and cruel dictatorship. Hussein's regime was clearly evil and dangerous, they argued, and its elimination would bring about a more stable Middle East and reduced support for terrorists.

The debates ebbed and flowed during the first weeks of the war. No clear answers came forth from the sandstorms, the fog of war, and the smoke from burning crude oil facilities.

10

THE TIDES OF WAR

Week 2

Over the period from March 27 though April 2, the war in Iraq increased in intensity, with Coalition forces continuing to make advances toward the capital. Working with close air support, U.S. Marines and the 3rd Infantry Division moved northward in a two-pronged attack toward Baghdad. By the end of the period they were on the outskirts of Baghdad and were poised to take the city's major airport just to the west of the city's center. Every day through this period, embedded reporters and media people back at Doha, Qatar, told of successful advances, destroyed targets, and victories by Coalition troops. Even so, analysts worried about the psychological aspects of the war: the morale of the troops and the response of the American public to casualty figures and to numerous incidents of continued violations of the conventions of war. Commanders and press officers tried to get the media to focus on the positives and not to dwell on the negatives. So the war moved forward on two fronts: not only on the ground in Iraq, but on the front of news reporting, news slant, and editorializing.

Although the Iraqis did not fire any long-range Scuds toward Israel in this war, as they had done in 1991, they did employ a few tactical missiles against U.S. positions, at first in Kuwait and later against the advancing troops inside Iraq. Generally, the missile attacks were not very successful. In one strike on March 27, Iraqis launched a short-range missile against Coalition installations in Kuwait, but the missile was knocked out by a Patriot surface-to-air missile, and soon after, U.S. Air Force A-10s destroyed the Iraqi launcher and several other vehicles. By

This Tomahawk cruise missile lifts off from a ship in the eastern Mediterranean Sea to hit a precise target in Iraq, more than 400 miles away. *(Intelligence Specialist 1st Class Kenneth Moll, Department of Defense)*

April 1, Patriots had shot down some eight missiles fired toward Kuwait, and then one was intercepted as it was fired against U.S. troops in Iraq. Three days later, British patrols outside Basra near the town of Al Zubair seized a cache of 56 surface-to-surface, short-range ballistic missiles and four missile launchers.

The ground battle reports revealed tough resistance that kept cropping up in spots that had been bypassed in the rapid advances. The U.S. 3rd Infantry Division approached Karbala, and to the south, other elements of the 3rd Infantry Division continued to fight Iraqi forces in An Najaf. The Iraqis encircled in An Najaf were estimated to total some 3,000 to 6,000 soldiers and irregular forces. Coalition aircraft struck the An Najaf Baath Party headquarters and some government sites there. Meanwhile, the eastern prong of the advance, headed by the 1st Marine Expeditionary Force, was thought to be several days behind schedule of the original plan due to the sandstorm as well as continued enemy resistance.

In southern Iraq, the British 3rd Commando Brigade held the Al Faw Peninsula, while their 7th Armored Brigade kept up a loose sort of siege of Basra. The British 16th Air Assault Brigade worked on securing the

U.S. Army trucks bring water and other supplies to assist the British in putting out the fires at the Rumaila oil field. *(Photographer's Mate 1st Class Arlo K. Abrahamson, Department of Defense)*

Rumaila oil field and facilities. On the morning of March 27, the Royal Scots Dragoon Guards using 14 Challenger medium battle tanks took on a roughly equal-sized Iraqi force of Russian-made T-55 tanks and destroyed 14 of the Iraqi tanks with no losses. At Umm Qasr, divers from the Australian navy and U.S. Navy forces cleared mines from the ship channel into the harbor. The British ship *Sir Galahad* stayed offshore due to the threat from the mined harbor. *Sir Galahad* carried relief supplies for the civilian population of southern Iraq and finally docked on March 28. Coalition forces took the Basra refinery, one of three major refinery complexes in Iraq, on March 28. In the north, in the Bani Maqan area close to Kirkuk, Kurdish forces occupied evacuated Iraqi positions without engaging in combat.

In several separate episodes, the complex crosscurrents of the war surfaced. On March 28, fighter-bombers reported attacking a site in Basra where some 200 Baath Party members had assembled. Meanwhile, in response to reports that Syria had shipped in night-vision goggles to Iraq and that Syrian volunteers were coming across the border to fight against Coalition troops, Secretary of Defense Rumsfeld warned other countries in the region not to provide any assistance to the Iraqi regime. In western Iraq, special operations forces attacked a group of 30 armed individuals who were wearing civilian clothes.

Several episodes in these days of the war showed the new nature of warfare and some of the unexpected types of threats. On March 29, the Iraqis fired a cruise missile that fell harmlessly into the sea and exploded near Kuwait's most popular shopping mall. Also on March 29, a suicide bomber set off explosives hidden in a taxi at a U.S. checkpoint near An Najaf, resulting in the death of four U.S. soldiers. It was the first such attack of the war, and the Iraqi regime promptly awarded two medals to the dead bomber. The Iraqis warned that further suicide attacks would be used against U.S. forces, who became much more cautious about vehicles at checkpoints.

Action continued both at the front and in the rear. Near An Nasiriyah, where marines had seized two crucial bridges, U.S. supply

Among the supplies brought in by the British ship *Sir Galahad* is bottled drinking water, off-loaded by crane at the port of Umm Qasr.
(Photographer's Mate 1st Class, Ronald V. Woxland, Department of Defense)

President George W. Bush and Secretary of Defense Donald Rumsfeld hold a hurried discussion in a Pentagon corridor regarding developments in Iraq. *(R. D. Ward, Department of Defense)*

convoys continued to encounter attacks from the Fedayeen Saddam. Most of the 3rd Infantry Division assembled between An Najaf and Karbala preparing for the final thrust into the capital. Although the 3rd Infantry tried to rest and refuel after the leapfrogging dash through the desert from Kuwait, many of its troops fought militiamen inside and near the two cities.

Analysts and commentators continued to debate whether the use of Baath Party militias, paramilitary forces, irregulars, and the more organized Fedayeen Saddam represented dedication on the part of the Iraqis to defend their homeland or the last dying gasp of a corrupt regime relying on a few die-hard and ill-equipped loyalists. When coupled with reports of terror tactics that surfaced in this period, these types of resistance showed that the Iraq War was not going to be a simple matter of defeating regular forces.

Episodes of terrorist-like tactics continued to show up. On March 30, in Kuwait, an Egyptian electrician steered a pickup truck into a group of U.S. soldiers who stood near a store, wounding 15. Kuwaiti police said the man, who was doing some work at the camp, appeared to have targeted the soldiers out of anger at the U.S.-British invasion of Iraq. Fourteen of the soldiers suffered only minor injuries that were treated locally; the

U.S. troops got a mixed reception in southern and central Iraq. Here, a soldier from the 422nd Civil Affairs Battalion speaks with a boy during the distribution of rice and wheat to the youth's village, near An Najaf. *(Staff Sergeant Kevin P. Bell, Department of Defense)*

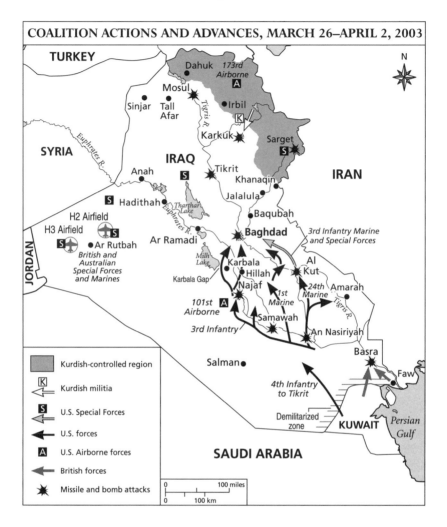

COALITION ACTIONS AND ADVANCES, MARCH 26–APRIL 2, 2003

other was flown to Germany for medical treatment of a more serious injury. U.S. and British soldiers who manned vehicle checkpoints in Iraq remained in a state of high alert implemented after the earlier suicide attack.

CENTCOM sought to suggest that the irregular troops and terrorists were not entirely representative of the Iraqi civilian population. Official reports showed that American troops sometimes encountered cases of widespread popular welcome, especially in smaller towns and villages in the lower Tigris and Euphrates river region. On April 1, the 1st Marine

Division mounted several raids into at least six towns and villages in the central Iraq area to liberate the local people and hunt down paramilitary groups and units. Local villagers gave the marines information on the locations and hideouts of Baath Party leaders, documents, and weapons caches. Some provided intelligence regarding regular army and paramilitary operations. The marines doled out humanitarian rations and medical assistance. Yet in the same south-central region, marines fought a difficult street-to-street engagement in and around the town of Ad Diwaniyah where they took some 20 Iraqi prisoners.

In effect, the war went on in three separate ways. At one level, air strikes continued against major command and control facilities and against targets of opportunity. In the main ground action, the two major groups, the Marine Expeditionary Force in the east and the army's 3rd Infantry Division in the west kept moving ahead in their leapfrog advances toward the capital. Meanwhile, in the rear, irregular forces continued to harass the supply lines for the advancing troops and to prevent the British from establishing firm control over the Basra region; various Coalition forces sought to suppress those activities. As a consequence, the day-by-day account of the war left a confusing impression of conflict scattered across nearly 300 miles of the country, with occasional bits of news coming from the northern front where the Kurds, supported by U.S. paratroopers, continued to pressure Iraqi forces.

U.S. ground forces kept up operations on March 30 around the four key cities to the south—An Nasiriyah, As Samawah, An Najaf, and Karbala—to defeat Iraqi army and paramilitary units threatening the transport convoys of U.S. troops moving north. American troops expected to encounter three Republican Guard divisions that defended the approaches to Baghdad: the Medina Division to the south, the Al Nida Division to the east, and the Baghdad Division around the city of Al Kut. Over the next few days, the U.S. troops did indeed engage the three Guard divisions as well as other regular Iraqi units and militia groups.

The front line units of the 3rd Infantry Division pushed to Al Hillah, southeast of Karbala, after overnight air strikes broke up three Iraqi army mechanized and tank units guarding the approach routes to the city. Iraqi troops identified as militiamen, equipped only with assault rifles and rocket-propelled grenade launchers, resisted the advance; however, they were pushed back by artillery and rockets, allowing elements of the 3rd Infantry to move up on the Republican Guard's Medina Division, which had taken up positions to the north of Karbala.

Republican Guard

BEFORE AND DURING OPERATION IRAQI FREEDOM, military analysts, planners, and the news media expected the strongest resistance by the Iraqi armed forces to come from several units known as the Republican Guard. These elite units, or "shock troops," represented the best-trained and best-paid units in the Iraqi military. In addition, they had the best equipment, including modern armored vehicles, self-propelled howitzer artillery pieces, and new towed artillery pieces from Austria. Almost all of the troops and officers in the Republican Guard were Sunni Arabs, rather than Kurds or Shiites.

When Saddam Hussein ordered the invasion of Kuwait in 1990, it was units of the Republican Guard who overran that small country. After the invasion, the Republican Guard units were pulled back and their places taken by regular army troops. Even so, in Operation Desert Storm of the Persian Gulf War, U.S. and Coalition troops sought out units of the Republican Guard within Iraq and inflicted severe casualties on them.

The Iraqi Republican Guard had its first combat experience in the long Iran-Iraq War (1980–88). It was during this period that the Republican Guard became an all-volunteer force, and units of the guard were victorious over the Iranians in some of the last battles of that war. Named after famous historic figures or geographical sites in Iraq, the six divisions of the Republican Guard reconstituted after the Persian Gulf War were as follows:

Armored	Infantry
Al Medina Division	Baghdad Division
Hammurabi Division	Adnan Division
Al Nida Division	Nebuchadnezzar Division

As originally organized, each division would have more than 11,000 men, but because of losses during the Persian Gulf War, most of the units had a maximum of about 8,000 troops. In addition, the numbers of tanks and artillery pieces originally planned for the units were at a reduced level by 2003. On the eve of Operation Iraqi Freedom, the remaining six divisions were organized into two corps, which in Iraq as in most armies, represent groups of divisions. The Northern Corps consisted of the Medina, Baghdad, and Adnan Divisions; the Southern Corps consisted of the Nebuchadnezzar, Hammurabi, and Al Nida Divisions.

In addition, there was a separate unit, known as the Special Republican Guard (SRG). The SRG was made up of two regiments of tanks, four brigades, and an air-defense command. Although all of the Republican Guard units had originally been planned as special units to protect Saddam Hussein and the government against internal coups or uprisings, fear that some of the units might themselves become involved in coup attempts led to the Northern and Southern Corps being stationed outside Baghdad. Only the Special Republican Guard, most of whose members were volunteers from the region around Tikrit, the homeland of Hussein and his family, were allowed inside the city. The overall commander of both the Republican Guard and the SRG was Hussein's son Qusay Saddam Hussein and the guard units were not subordinate to the Defense Ministry, but to the State Special Security Apparatus.

Outside experts culled through reports of defectors and communications information to determine whether the Republican Guard and SRG forces would represent a dangerous threat to Coalition forces during Operation Iraqi Freedom. Opinions varied. Some analysts feared that the guard units would fall back into Baghdad and conduct a street-to-street and even house-to-house defense that would be very dangerous for advancing U.S. troops. Others believed that, even with their superior training and equipment, the guard units would be no match for regular U.S. troops, let alone for highly trained combat units such as the marines and the army's 3rd Infantry Division. As it turned out, units of the Republican Guard mounted some of the strongest resistance to U.S. advances.

Iraqi president Saddam Hussein talks with elite Republican Guard officers in Baghdad on March 1, 2003, shortly before the start of the Iraq War. *(Reuters/Landov)*

Meanwhile, important actions continued further to the south. In An Najaf the 1st Brigade of the 101st Airborne Division used artillery and air strikes to target militiamen who mounted repeated attacks on U.S. military supply lines. In As Samawah, 50 miles south along the Euphrates River, two battalions from the 82nd Airborne Division fought an estimated 1,000 paramilitary fighters. A marine raid in An Nasiriyah took over several buildings that had been held by the Iraqi 11th Infantry Division.

With operations both at the advancing front and in the rear, all of them reported rather vaguely by embedded reporters who usually did not even name the towns they were near, few except the military commanders had any clear picture of what was going on. The front line reports could have been more explicit, but reporters usually kept them quite general in order to withhold vital information from the enemy. In one incident, television personality Geraldo Rivera, who was not formally

This boy has just received a "humanitarian daily ration" package from troops with the 82nd Airborne Division, outside the city of As Samawah. *(Staff Sergeant Eric Foltz, Department of Defense)*

Hunt for Weapons of Mass Destruction

ALTHOUGH BOTH THE BRITISH AND AMERICANS CON-
tinued to search for poison gas or other weapons of mass destruction
(WMD), during the actual combat they found only chemical defensive
gear. Central Command reported that marines had found some 300
chemical suits and masks; injectors for a poison nerve gas antidote,
atropine; two decontamination vehicles, and other decontamination
equipment all at one site. At another location, they uncovered a conventional arms cache of more than 800 rocket-propelled grenades,
hundreds of mortar and artillery rounds, mines, and large amounts of
small arms ammunition. In Basra, British troops uncovered a stash of
training equipment for chemical warfare. Among the items were a
Geiger counter, nerve gas simulators, gas masks, and protective suits. A
week later, on April 4, U.S. Army Special Forces took over a site in western Iraq near Mudaysis that indicated that it had been used at some
time as a nuclear, biological, and chemical warfare training center for
the Iraqi army. All of these finds were suggestive; they did not confirm
the prewar intelligence estimates presented by Secretary of State Colin
Powell to the United Nations Security Council that the Hussein regime
was well equipped with WMDs.

For critics of the war, the failure to locate evidence of WMDs represented proof that the war had been started on false premises. For supporters of the war, the failure to locate such weapons only demonstrated
that the Iraqis had been extremely careful to conceal them or to remove
them from the country entirely.

embedded among the troops but rather was visiting a unit, sketched out
a rough map in the sand showing the advance for the television camera.
He was severely criticized by some of his colleagues for the apparent
breach of security, although others said that no Iraqi officer would treat
such information as reliable or accurate.

Air strikes continued, with more and more of them targeting the
Republican Guard. There were approximately 2,000 sorties flown on
March 31. While some sorties were aimed against assigned targets, most
went for emerging targets in the Republican Guard—that is, using rapidly
relayed intelligence, the pilots would seek out units of the Republican
Guard as they moved. In other air war action, fighter aircraft from Carrier

Air Wing 8, based aboard USS *Theodore Roosevelt* in the Mediterranean, hit targets in northern Iraq through the night of March 31. There, pilots flew nearly 50 sorties against artillery installations, a barracks, and a surface-to-air-missile installation. The missions had the purpose of increasing the pressure on ground forces and supporting the 173rd Airborne Brigade in that region.

At the end of March, reports were still coming from actions along the supply route. The 3rd Infantry Division captured a bridge over the Euphrates River near Al Handiyah, sparing a crucial piece of Iraqi infrastructure that Iraqi forces had planned to demolish. Both the British and the Americans continued to insist that they hoped to prevent damage to such facilities, whether caused by their own attacks or by the Iraqis as they retreated so that there would be less difficulty in reconstructing the country after the war. Engineers with the 2nd Brigade Combat Team cleared away the explosives on the Al Handiyah bridge and reported that it was safe for travel. The 101st Airborne Division attacked and took over the airfield at An Najaf, trying to isolate enemy units in the area. The division destroyed two T-55 tanks, as well as 15 pickup trucks with mounted

While forces advanced from the south, troops from the 173rd Airborne Brigade dropped in and secured an airfield in northern Iraq, supported by aircraft carrier–based planes from the Mediterranean Sea. *(PFC Brandon Aird, Department of Defense)*

weapons known as technical vehicles, or technicals. The airborne troops also knocked out a field artillery battery in the same operation.

New waves of Coalition bombing crossed Iraq, and foreign journalists reported more large explosions in Baghdad early on April 1 in some of the heaviest air raids since the first days of the war. Even so, there was no suggestion that the Iraqi forces or government were about to surrender. Other air strikes continued to target Republican Guard units that stood in the way of the southern approaches to Baghdad.

In the midst of these mixed reports, some good, some bad, the U.S. forces came up with a startling, positive piece of news. In a daring raid, special operations forces had rescued one of the prisoners from the 507th Maintenance Company, the unit that had been captured on March 23, Jessica Lynch. The story received front-page coverage across the United States and much of the world, and segments of the rescue action, filmed in the ghostly green light of night-vision equipment, were broadcast and rebroadcast to fascinated audiences. Almost from the day of the rescue, however, mysterious elements and controversies swirled around the report, raising questions about exactly what had happened.

Early in the morning of April 2, reporters were summoned to a briefing with General Brooks in Doha, Qatar. There, he announced that some U.S. troops had put their lives on the line in the tradition of leaving no fallen soldier behind. They had raided, under defending gunfire, a hospital near An Nasiriyah where Private Lynch was being held. The film clip of the episode, rapidly prepared for distribution, was shown and copies provided to the media. According to the information released by CENTCOM, a courageous Iraqi attorney had come forward with information as to Lynch's whereabouts, in a hospital used as a base for the Fedayeen Saddam.

Later, interviews with the hospital staff revealed a somewhat different story. Two days before the raid, an ambulance driver had attempted to deliver Private Lynch to the American lines but had been turned back by gunfire at a checkpoint. By the time of the raid, the Fedayeen had abandoned the hospital, leaving only doctors, nurses, and a few patients. When the U.S. troops arrived, they fired blanks, broke down doors, and shouted to everyone to get down. Jessica herself heard the troops in the hall, asking loudly "Where is Jessica Lynch?" She feared that they were Iraqis come to take her to another location. When they burst in her room, she could not at first make out their uniforms. One removed his helmet so she could see him clearly as he told her they were U.S. soldiers

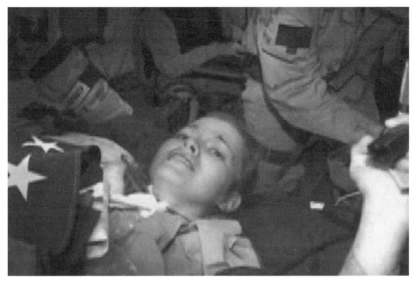

Freed during a dramatic raid on the hospital where she was held as a prisoner of war, Private First Class Jessica Lynch told her rescuers, "I'm an American soldier, too." *(Department of Defense)*

and that they had come to take her to safety. She replied, in a line that became a classic, "I'm an American soldier, too."

Critics of the U.S. style of handling the press later claimed that the raid had been overdramatized and that the film had been carefully edited to give it an action-movie feel. CENTCOM and the Defense Department had wanted a story that would lift morale as the war seemed to drag on, and the rescue of Private Lynch was just such a story, they claimed. The CENTCOM press officer and representative of the White House on the scene, Jim Wilkinson, had engineered the ultimate media event, they suggested.

Others pointed out some facts that contradicted claims of a staged operation. Although the team of navy Seals and army Rangers had intelligence that the Fedayeen had abandoned the hospital, they had often been confronted with false information and at the moment of attack could not be sure if the information was accurate. The diversionary detonations they set off were designed not to add drama but to distract any possible defenders. Although they encountered only medical staff and patients in the hospital, many Iraqi regulars and irregular troops had already dressed in civilian clothes and had used concealed weapons. To avoid any chance of casualties during the raid, the team had to assume the worst and treat everyone as a potential "hostile."

Long after the main combat phase of the war ended, analysts, historians, and television documentary producers continued to debate whether members of the press had willingly allowed themselves to be manipulated because the rescue made a good news story. Lynch, who had very little memory of the events between her capture and her rescue, worked with writers to present her side of the whole episode. In her statements, she criticized the media for blowing her capture and her rescue out of proportion.

However, on April 2, as the rescue was publicized around the world, the drama of the event did seem to lift the spirits of the troops and the American public. The war was over for Private Lynch, but the other American troops were poised for their push into Baghdad.

11

BATTLING PAST BAGHDAD

By April 2, U.S. forces had moved within about 35 miles of the southern outskirts of Baghdad. The advance on Baghdad came as a kind of grand pincer movement from the southwest and the southeast. From the southwest, U.S. Army units rolled past Republican Guard positions west of Karbala and gained control of a nearby dam. Coalition commanders and media analysts alike had feared that Iraqis would sabotage the dam and flood the region, blocking the advance of Coalition troops. In general, the defending Iraqi forces did far less demolition of infrastructure than the Coalition planners had anticipated.

From the southeast, near the city of Al Kut, U.S. Marines virtually eliminated the Baghdad Division of the Republican Guard and took an important bridge over the Tigris River near Al Kut. With the way around Al Kut cleared and the bridge over the Tigris opened, the marines were ready to advance from the southeast while the army pushed toward Baghdad from the direction of the Karbala Gap on the southwest.

Even as the U.S. forces moved into the Baghdad suburbs from both directions, resistance continued in the rear, with attacks on supply lines and in isolated pockets. In An Najaf, one Iraqi unit continued to fire on Coalition troops with impunity because they were holed up in the Ali Mosque, a gold-domed structure reputed to be the burial place of Ali, Muhammad's son-in-law. In accordance with established conventions of war, U.S. and British forces had ruled all such holy sites in Iraq off limits for attack.

Over April 2 to April 3, the 3rd Infantry Division captured part of Saddam International Airport on the western outskirts of Baghdad. After moving through the Karbala Gap and seizing a bridge over the Euphrates River at Yasin al Khudayr on April 2, the division's 1st Brigade Combat Team pushed into the outskirts of Baghdad on April 3. Even as the sound of fighting could be heard, the Iraqi information minister, Mohammed Saeed al-Sahaf, gave impromptu press conferences denying that U.S. troops were anywhere near the city, a topic of ridicule by cartoonists and editorial writers in the United States. Soon, American comedians referred to him as "Baghdad Bob" and delighted in directly quoting his denials.

Approaching the airport, C Company of the 2nd Battalion, 7th Infantry took on two companies of Republican Guard forces. Apparently the U.S. troops caught the Iraqi defenders by surprise. Tanks of Task Force (TF) 3-69 broke through the perimeter of the airport at about 7:30 P.M., local time, on April 3. While TF 3-69 and other elements of the 1st Brigade Combat Team started to clear the airport from the western side, artillery and aircraft hit Iraqi positions on the eastern edges of the airport complex. The Iraqis mounted a force to defend the airport, a force estimated to include two tank battalions, two mechanized infantry battalions, and two infantry battalions. The battle for the airport was one of the hardest fought of the war, yet one with very few casualties to the U.S. troops.

To the south of Baghdad, other units continued security operations and the elimination of Iraqi positions bypassed by the initial thrusts of the army and marine forces. The 101st Airborne Division kept fighting around An Najaf, trying to eliminate pockets of Iraqi resistance, while the 2nd Brigade of the 82nd Airborne Division struck at intelligence and paramilitary sites in As Samawah. The air attacks against command and control targets continued, with Coalition forces hitting Iraqi air force headquarters facilities in central Baghdad, located just west of the Tigris River, near the Muthenna military airport.

During the night of April 3–4, elements of the 1st Brigade Combat Team, 3rd Infantry Division completed the capture of Saddam International Airport, which they promptly renamed Baghdad International Airport. As the U.S. troops cleared the runways and surrounding buildings and tunnels, they encountered a large Iraqi force at about 4:30 A.M., April 4. In one engagement, two companies of TF 3-69 took on Iraqi Special Republican Guard forces on the east side of the airfield. Fighting

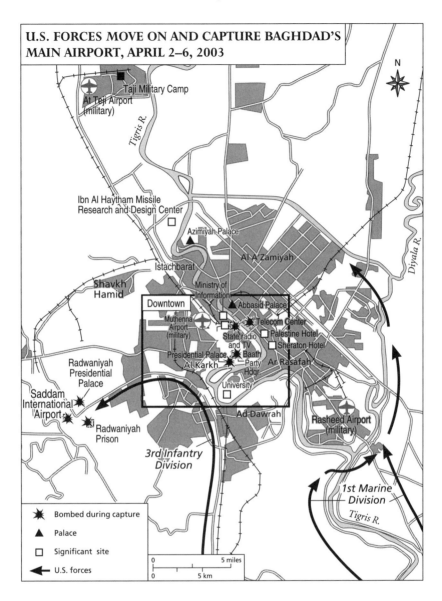

U.S. FORCES MOVE ON AND CAPTURE BAGHDAD'S MAIN AIRPORT, APRIL 2–6, 2003

kept up for three hours, resulting in 250 Special Republican Guard killed and three tanks destroyed. Over about 12 hours of the airport battle, U.S. forces suffered only one dead and eight wounded.

From the southeast, the 1st Marine Expeditionary Force also continued its approach on Baghdad, destroying surviving elements of the

Baghdad Republican Guard Division near Al Kut, and troops from the Al Nida Republican Guard Division between Al Kut and Baghdad. About 2,500 Republican Guard soldiers surrendered to the marines in the area near Al Kut, in what was apparently the largest single surrender of Iraqi troops of the whole war up to that date.

On April 5, two battalion-size task forces of the 3rd Infantry Division raided downtown Baghdad. The force drove into the city from the south and reached the Tigris River in the central zone of palaces and government buildings. As international journalists stationed in the downtown hotels photographed the passing armored vehicles of the U.S. troops, the picture was confusing. After all, there was no street-to-street fighting in Baghdad and the U.S. forces seemed able to move about freely, but somehow, the war was not over. The task force then withdrew to the west to link up with elements of the 1st Brigade Combat Team at the recently renamed Baghdad International Airport. Other Coalition forces pressed forward near As Suwayrah, southwest of Baghdad. CENTCOM reported that U.S. units had destroyed the Republican Guard's Division Medina headquarters in that area and reported the breakup of the Republican Guard Adnan Division as well. Meanwhile, the 24th Marine Expeditionary Unit continued attempts at pacification and convoy security in southern Iraq. By April 5, only a little more than three full weeks into the war, about 2,500 vehicles moved regularly along a 350-mile supply line connecting forward forces with their supply bases in Kuwait.

With American troops on the outskirts of Baghdad and moving into and through the city, it seemed the war was ready to wind down. As part of the attempt to end the regime, two Coalition aircraft using laser-guided munitions struck the Basra residence of Ali Hassan al-Majid, Saddam Hussein's cousin. Al-Majid had become notorious for ordering the use of chemical weapons on Kurds in northern Iraq and was known to the media and the public as "Chemical Ali." He held the formal title of commander of the Southern Forces and had been assigned the King of Spades in the famous deck of cards. The next day, British forces mistakenly reported they had recovered al-Majid's body. He was later captured alive.

As U.S. forces moved into Baghdad, they encountered no central Iraqi commanding officers who offered to formally surrender either the city or the country as a whole, and numerous skirmishes and pitched battles continued over the next three weeks, in a gradual winding-down of the war. Formal national surrender in other wars had several important functions. Perhaps most important, a surrender could serve as a notice to the defending troops to lay down their weapons and to avoid unnecessary sacrifice on their part. In Iraq, the leadership was apparently unconcerned with death rates even when all military resistance was futile. The absence of a formal surrender made the situation difficult for the Coalition forces in several ways. Not only was it nearly impossible to state with certainty when the war ended, but Coalition troops continued to suffer casualties long after it was clear that the regime of Saddam Hussein no longer governed Iraq. By April 6, the Coalition was able to land the first of many flights at the Baghdad International Airport.

Even as the defeat of Iraq seemed imminent, acts of sabotage, armed resistance, and friendly-fire casualties continued. On April 4, three U.S. military personnel were fatally wounded by a car bomb at a checkpoint about 11 miles southeast of the Hidathah Dam in western Iraq. The soldiers had approached the car in response to the apparent distress of one of the passengers, who they later said seemed to be a pregnant woman. As the troops neared the car there was a large explosion. The woman and a man in the vehicle were killed along with three soldiers, while two other people nearby were wounded.

Meanwhile, in a friendly-fire incident in northern Iraq, a U.S. aircraft mistakenly attacked a convoy of Kurdish fighters and U.S. Special Forces troops. Some 18 of the Kurdish troops were killed and more than 40 wounded, including the younger brother of Massoud Barzani, one of the leaders of the Kurdistan Democratic Party.

Working on information that Hussein and his two sons were attending a meeting at a home in the Al Mansour section of Baghdad, a B1-B bomber dropped four 2000-pound bombs on the property, at about 2:00 in the afternoon of April 7. The bomb destroyed at least three buildings and left a crater more than 50 feet deep. Over the next few days, unsuccessful efforts were made to determine whether Hussein or other important individuals had been killed in the attack, but sources on the ground indicated that the meeting had broken up shortly before the bombing.

On April 7 and 8, forces of the 3rd Infantry Division took up positions in downtown Baghdad, making it clear that they intended to stay, not just conduct a temporary raid. More than 100 armored vehicles took up positions around the Republican Palace and other government facilities in the downtown section. Some of the fighting for these positions was heavy, and the army reported that an estimated 600 Iraqi soldiers and paramilitary troops were killed in the actions.

For the first time in decades, Iraqis were able to hold public protests against authorities. Here, a demonstration opposes the reinstatement of police officers from the former regime in mid-April 2003. *(Staff Sergeant Kevin P. Bell, Department of Defense)*

In southern Iraq, British forces announced that they finally had control of Basra after the siege that had lasted about two weeks. British forces entered the center of the city on April 8. With the port of Umm Qasr open, more relief supplies began to flow into southern Iraq.

The final linkup of army and marine troops on April 9 required some hard fighting and led to several surprises. As U.S. Marine forces approached Baghdad, they encountered Iraqi forces trying to blow up bridges ahead of them and during one of the crossings of the Diyala River, two marines were killed and three wounded when their amphibious vehicle was hit by an Iraq shell. On April 8, U.S. Army forces in downtown Baghdad held the west bank of the Tigris River and faced an Iraqi counterattack that came from the east bank of the river. Iraqi troops crossed bridges in buses and trucks, as well as in several armored personnel carriers. The 3rd Infantry Division fought off the attacks, and several hundred Iraqis were estimated as killed. On the same day, two journalists were killed and several were injured when a round thought to be fired from a U.S. tank struck the Palestine Hotel, the headquarters for numerous foreign journalists. In a separate incident, a third journalist

Al-Jazeera

THE SATELLITE TELEVISION NEWS CHANNEL AL-JAZEERA was created in the 1990s by Arab newsmen and journalists who had formerly worked for the British Broadcasting Corporation (BBC). When they found their reporting censored by the Saudi Arabian government, they sought another outlet. Funded by the emir of Qatar and other Arab moderates, the network prides itself on broadcasting both sides of a story. The channel came to the attention of the world's media when it broadcast tapes from Osama bin Laden in October 2001, during the short war against the Taliban regime in Afghanistan. The U.S. government believed that the taped messages could have contained coded instructions to al-Qaeda members and tried to discourage the broadcasts.

Following that controversy, al-Jazeera often angered not only the American government but also many Middle Eastern governments for broadcasting reports that identified corruption or that released information that was contrary to the official news slant of some local regimes. The al-Jazeera bureaus that gather news in Egypt, Syria, and Saudi Arabia have often been shut down for short periods as punishment for their independence. When the channel's agency in Iraq was bombed and an al-Jazeera reporter killed, many observers jumped to the conclusion that the attack was intentional.

with al-Jazeera television was killed when a U.S. air raid bombed the station's Baghdad bureau. Despite an outcry from the press, U.S. military officials denied that the incidents had been intentional, and they justified the firing on the Palestine Hotel as a response to small-arms and rocket-propelled-grenade fire that came from the building. Four days later, after an investigation by CENTCOM, the army concluded that there was no violation of the rules of engagement. Some witnesses claimed that the shot fired into the hotel might not have come from a tank at all.

The two approaching units, the 1st Marine Division from the southeast and the army's 3rd Infantry Division from the southwest, linked up in downtown Baghdad on April 9, representing the culmination of the pincer movement on the capital. As they moved into the city, U.S. soldiers assisted in tearing down a large statue of Hussein, in a scene that was videotaped and televised around the world. A small crowd of celebrating Iraqis gave the picture a symbolic flavor of liberation that was later rebroadcast many times to represent the end of the regime; however, fighting continued.

Newspapers and television stations around the world headlined the "Fall of Baghdad" on April 10. One curious indicator of the Coalition victory in the capital was that none of the Iraqi employees of government ministries showed up for work on April 9, not even Baghdad Bob, the information minister. In the United States, even newspapers that had developed an editorial position opposing the war or critical of its execution hailed the fall of the city as a defining moment of victory. Many featured stories and pictures of groups of Iraqi citizens celebrating their liberation from the Hussein regime. Although the capital seemed to be in U.S. control by April 9 and 10, three important cities remained under Iraqi military control: Tikrit, Kirkuk, and Mosul—the first of these three being within what has been dubbed the "Sunni Triangle," the stronghold of Saddam Hussein's supporters.

Meanwhile, scattered engagements continued in areas already bypassed by the invading Coalition forces. For example, units of the 101st Airborne Division conducted operations in the city of Al Hillah against

Sunni Triangle

THE REGION KNOWN AS THE SUNNI TRIANGLE LIES TO the north and northwest of Baghdad. The triangle is formed roughly by imaginary lines connecting Baghdad, the two cities of Al Fallujah and Ar Ramadi to the west, and Tikrit to the north. This region of Iraq contains many towns and villages populated almost entirely by Sunni Muslim, Arabic-speaking Iraqis—the religious and ethnic group most loyal to the Hussein regime. It is no coincidence that Hussein's native village of Auja lies within this triangle and that many of the top officials in his regime came from here, too. Beyond this triangular heartland, to the northwest along the Euphrates River and north along the Tigris River toward Mosul, there are many Sunni-majority communities, forming a larger triangle-shaped section of Iraq. As the Iraqi government collapsed, observers believed that the strongest resistance to Coalition forces would be encountered in the Sunni Triangle heartland area, and their predictions proved correct over the next year.

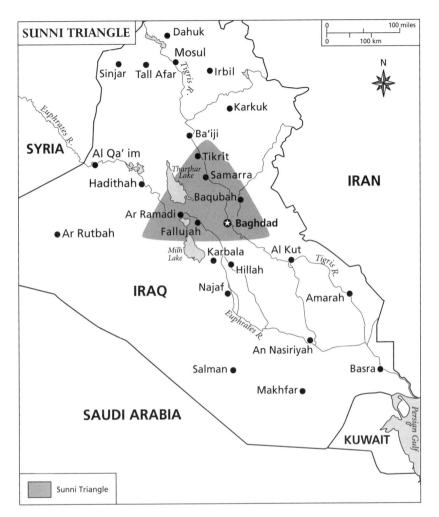

Iraqi irregular forces. In that city, a force estimated at 200 fighters engaged U.S. troops with automatic weapons and rocket-propelled grenades, along with several Iraqi tanks. The U.S. attack moved through Al Hillah with armor and close air support, capturing large caches of arms and ammunition. In northern Iraq, a combined U.S.-Kurdish force, including some units of the 173rd Airborne Brigade, entered the city of Kirkuk on April 10 and took control of nearby oil wells and a military airport.

It soon became clear that military control of Baghdad did not mean that U.S. forces could maintain order. Throughout the downtown region, looters stripped government buildings and palaces, taking everything, including desks, chairs, filing cabinets, and even electric and plumbing fixtures. On April 11 and for the following weeks, unrestrained looting continued on the streets of Baghdad and Kirkuk, despite sporadic army and marine force patrols to discourage it. The looting was so widespread that commanders did not give orders to shoot obvious looters. In a period of 48 hours, some 100,000 artifacts were taken from the Iraqi National Museum, including many rare and precious remnants of the ancient civilizations of Mesopotamia, although it eventually turned out that some of the most valuable objects had been placed in storage by Iraqi museum staff prior to the war. Some of the theft appeared to be the work of professional criminals who sought out the most valuable items for black market sale. There was international criticism that U.S. forces should have done more to protect the museum and other cultural institutions, or should have had a preventive plan in place.

Military operations reported from widely separated areas of Iraq gave an impression that the Coalition was establishing some form of control. British forces kept up security patrols in Basra and other nearby towns in southern Iraq. After a surrender of the Iraqi army's V Corps in

After Kurdish forces and units of the U.S. 173rd Airborne Brigade entered Kirkuk, a week of intense looting by Iraqis kept the city in turmoil. Later, these troops from the 1st Infantry Division came to help restore order. *(Private 1st Class Brandon R. Aird, Department of Defense)*

northern Iraq, U.S. Special Operations Forces met only scattered resistance from irregular forces as they moved into Mosul. In the north, the Bashur airfield began to receive regular flights of cargo aircraft, delivering millions of pounds of supplies. In western Iraq, at Al Qaim, Coalition special operations forces took over several facilities, including a railroad station, an air defense headquarters, some factories, and a water treatment plant. The troops reported finding two drone aircraft at a phosphate plant, which some reporters suspected had been planned for use in chemical attacks. Coalition special operations forces moved into Al Asad Airfield, where they found 15 airplanes concealed beneath camouflage, in undamaged condition. At one checkpoint in the west, Coalition special forces halted a bus carrying 59 military-age men apparently trying to leave the country. They were all taken as prisoners when it was found they were carrying letters offering rewards for killing American soldiers and a total of $630,000 in 100-dollar bills.

On April 12, 24 days after the beginning of combat, U.S. Marine forces moved out of Baghdad toward the north. Known as Task Force Tripoli, their objective was Tikrit, the last city under control of the Hussein regime. Rumors told of Tikrit harboring remnants of the Adnan Division of the Republican Guard and the presence of paramilitary forces in the general region. Meanwhile, the marines established control of Al Kut, the city that they had skirted around in their rush to the capital.

Even as the regular resistance by large units of Iraqi troops diminished, resistance in the form of irregular and terrorist activity remained a threat. For example, on the eastern side of Baghdad, on April 12, a marine guarding a hospital near the Tigris River was shot and killed by two men. Marines in Baghdad found 310 vests that were lined with explosives, clearly ready to be used by suicide bombers.

On April 13, as U.S. forces pushed toward Tikrit, troops of the 34th Marine Expeditionary Unit recovered seven American prisoners of war (POWs): two Apache helicopter pilots and five members of the 507th Maintenance Company, including Specialist Shoshana Johnson, who had been captured at the same time as Private Jessica Lynch. The group of POWs had been released by their captors and were simply walking beside a road outside Samarra, about 110 miles north of Baghdad. The American troops were led to the prisoners by Iraqi troops who had been abandoned by their commanders. As the news reached the families of the prisoners in the United States, national media reported on local celebrations in Georgia, New Jersey, New Mexico, Texas, and Kansas.

One of the members of 507th Maintenance Company captured by the enemy, Specialist Shoshana Johnson waves from a stretcher after her rescue, on her way to a hospital in Ramstein, Germany. *(Tech. Sergeant Maria L. Taylor, Department of Defense)*

Task Force Tripoli met little resistance advancing through Samarra and Baqubah. Approaching Tikrit from the south, west, and north, the marines entered Tikrit on April 13 and announced the next day that they had control of the city. Tikrit and the nearby small village of Auja, Hussein's hometown, were both heavily fortified and reportedly defended by about 2,500 regular and paramilitary troops. The estimates of the size of the defending force may have been exaggerated by the defenders themselves; however, air and ground attacks pounded the Iraqi positions, and the Iraqi soldiers reportedly ran away, leaving behind weapons and uniforms as they fled the Coalition advance. The marines destroyed four Iraqi tanks in the battles around Tikrit.

As American troops moved into Baghdad and then into the region around Tikrit, they found and occupied some of the reputed 49 palaces that Hussein had built for himself. Like Islamic emperors of an earlier era, Hussein ordered palaces constructed in every provincial town of

Iraq. Surprised and sometimes amused at the gaudiness of the palaces, embedded journalists and the troops themselves sat in golden armchairs, tried out the swimming pools, and photographed the buildings' interiors and exteriors. For a number of reasons, the palaces seemed to symbolize both the decadence and the tragedy of the Hussein regime.

The sheer quantity and bad taste of the palaces gave some insight into the personality of Iraq's dictator. While many in his country starved or suffered in extreme poverty, Hussein had surrounded himself with luxuries in the form of marble and alabaster floors, gold-plated bathroom fixtures, 20-foot high ceilings, wall paintings of Hussein himself, and lavish furnishings. The seizure of Hussein's personal homes seemed to symbolize very clearly the fall of the regime. The pictures of the troops inside the palaces, and others of the abandoned mansions overlooking a shattered landscape, showed the world that Hussein's personal regime had collapsed.

During the earlier inspection work of UNSCOM and UNMOVIC, the inspectors had often been denied access to the palaces and their compounds. The inspectors believed some palace compounds housed many of the records of the WMD programs, if not actual workshops and factories. But as the troops occupied the buildings in April 2003, they

Saddam Hussein had these hometown palaces. *(Lance Corporal Nicholous Radloff, Department of Defense)*

In the last combat phase of the war, U.S. Marines moved on Tikrit, where Marines approach one of the lavish palaces maintained by Hussein. The contrast with the poverty of many Iraqis was striking. *(Sergeant Nicholas S. Hizer, Department of Defense)*

found empty rooms, standing in quiet testimony to Hussein's ego. It became clear that some of the palaces had served as guesthouses and conference centers for visiting dignitaries. Under some of the palaces, the empty tunnels and bunkers seemed less like escape routes or hiding places and more like empty storage rooms.

Even though President Bush would not announce the formal end of the "combat phase of the war" until May 1, 2003, in effect all formal resistance to the Coalition forces by large regular Iraqi units ended with the fall of Tikrit and the surrounding area on April 14. Regular flights carrying personnel, equipment, and humanitarian supplies began to come into Baghdad International Airport. In Baghdad and other major cities in central and southern Iraq, Coalition forces began efforts to restore utilities, including electric power, and to set up police service. In addition to joint patrols with Iraqi civilian volunteers to try to control looting, ethnic clashes, terror attacks, and everyday crimes, U.S., British, and Australian special forces continued to search for leaders from Hussein's regime and for WMDs. With Hussein in hiding, his regime dissolved, and all regular units of the Iraqi army defeated or vanished, the war seemed to be over. Yet, the country was not at peace.

12

RESTORING ORDER

In the period from the end of April through the early summer of 2003, the occupying forces in Iraq dealt with lawlessness and disruption of all civil services. Looting, power outages, and unsteady water supply plagued not only Baghdad but also many of the smaller

One of the first duties of arriving Coalition troops was to provide drinking water for Iraqi civilians. Here, U.S. troops of the 486th Civil Affairs Company distribute water from a supply truck in a village near An Nasiriyah. *(Staff Sergeant Quinton T. Burris, Department of Defense)*

Immediately after the defeat of the Iraqi army, Shiite Muslims were free, for the first time in decades, to conduct a pilgrimage to the city of Karbala in honor of the grandson of the Prophet Muhammad. Many of the same pilgrims demanded the withdrawal of Coalition forces from Iraq. *(Landov)*

cities of Iraq. As summer temperatures rose to over 120 degrees Fahrenheit during the day, the lack of electricity for air-conditioning compounded the frustration of ordinary civilians in Baghdad. Some with private electric generators would rig lines to help friends or relatives in nearby buildings run air conditioners and to provide lighting, leaving the night sky over the city oddly illuminated in one neighborhood but pitch-dark in others. For most, however, it was simply too hot to sleep indoors, and they pulled their mattresses into courtyards and onto roofs to try to catch a few hours of rest, despite the roar of generators down the street.

More serious from the point of view of British and U.S. troops were the low-level attacks by irregular forces that injured or killed as many as 10 soldiers a week. The attacks ranged from small engagements of a few irregulars with a detachment of occupying troops, to assassinations of individual soldiers by rifle fire, to incidents of rocket-propelled grenades fired at vehicles. Other attacks took the form of explosive devices planted next to a road and detonated remotely when a Coalition vehicle passed by.

Although President Bush had announced on May 1, 2003, that the combat phase of the war was over, the continued casualty rates made it

Deck of Cards

OF THE 55 MOST WANTED, AS DISPLAYED IN THE DECK of cards issued by the Coalition, the following had been taken into custody or surrendered before May 1, 2003:

Queen of Spades—Muhammad Hamza al-Zubaydi (April 20)
Queen of Diamonds—Muzahim Sab Hasan al-Tikriti (April 23)
Nine of Clubs—Jamal Mustafa Abdallah Sultan al-Tikriti (April 20)
Eight of Spades—Tariq Aziz (April 25)
Eight of Diamonds—Hikmat Mizban Ibrahim al-Assawi (April 18)
Eight of Clubs—Walid Hamid Tawfiq al-Tikriti (April 29)
Seven of Hearts—Zuhayr Talib abd al-Sattqar al Naqib (April 23)
Seven of Diamonds—Amir Hamudi Hasan al-Sadi (April 12)
Six of Spades—Amir Muhammad Rashid al-Tikriti al-Ubaydi
(April 28)

Six of Hearts—Muhammed Mahdi al-Salih (April 23)
Six of Clubs—Hussan Muhammad Amin al-Yasin (April 27)
Five of Spades—Watban Ibrahim Hassan al-Tikriti (April 13)
Five of Clubs—Barzan Ibrahim Hassan al-Tikriti (April 16)
Four of Hearts—Humam abd al-Khaliq abd al-Ghafur (April 19)
Four of Clubs—Samir abd al-Aziz al-Najim (April 17)

seem that the war was still ongoing. During the period March 20–April 30, about 115 American troops had been killed, and such losses were immense tragedies to the families of those killed, but from the perspective of historical comparison, no U.S. military campaign to defeat an enemy and conquer as large a territory as Iraq had ever been conducted with so few casualties. Nevertheless, as the summer wore on, it became clear that the number of casualties during the military occupation of Iraq would soon exceed those suffered during the combat phase. By September 2003, the number of American soldiers killed in Iraq since the official end of regular combat had passed the number killed between March 20 and May 1.

Despite the casualties, in the first weeks following the end of combat, there were some signs of progress. For the first time in decades, Shiite Muslims were able to conduct a pilgrimage to Karbala, the location of the shrine to Muhammad's grandson who was killed as a martyr in the seventh century, and to An Najaf, the burial shrine of Imam Ali, son-in-law of Muhammad. Both shrines are holy sites for the Shiite branch of the Islamic religion, and Hussein had banned pilgrimages to both locations. The ability to openly practice the Shiite faith could be viewed as one of the first signs that Iraq was being rapidly transformed into a state that allowed freedom of religion along the lines of Western democracies. The pilgrimages, estimated in the press to involve up to 2 million people, flowed openly in the week of April 20–27.

One by one, some of the lower-ranking members of Hussein's regime represented on the famous deck of cards were either arrested or turned themselves in to the occupying forces for questioning. Even before President Bush declared an end to the conflict on May 1, 15 of the most wanted had been captured. The number apprehended mounted almost every week through the summer.

Such promising signs, however, were offset by elements of disturbing news. The leading Shiite religious figures, who had opposed Hussein's regime, now seemed ready to oppose U.S. occupation. Although liberated from the repression of religious expression imposed by Hussein, the Shiites were highly vocal in opposition to the influence of the West and to what they saw as cultural insensitivity on the part of the occupying troops. It soon became clear that some of the Shiite leaders hoped to establish a religious state, similar to that in Iran or to the former Taliban regime in Afghanistan, that would control the daily life of everyone in the country. Their liberation, it seemed, was capable of leading to a state that would deny liberty to others.

Shiite Resurgence

U.S. INTELLIGENCE REPORTS IN THE FIRST DAYS AFTER the end of formal combat indicated that the Shiite regime in Iran was funding new clinics and religious schools, known as madrassas, in Iraq. In one section of Baghdad formerly known as Saddam City, Shiites renamed their neighborhood Sadr City, after a Shiite clergyman Mohammed Sadiq al-Sadr, who was murdered by the Hussein regime in 1995. In the heart of the sprawling slum of some 2 million people, the imams, or religious leaders, set up their own civilian police force to protect against looting. Under the direction of Sheik Hussein al-Assadi, who made his headquarters in Sadr Hospital, citizens returned stolen goods and turned in thieves. But the establishment of some degree of local order under such leadership was hardly encouraging to the occupying forces.

The lack of water supply and electricity in the slum only worsened conditions. Various imams broadcast anti-American slogans and speeches from loudspeakers mounted on the mosques of Sadr City, powered by gasoline and diesel generators. Unemployed young men and boys stood in groups in the litter-filled streets, listening to the speeches.

The head of the community was Muqtada al-Sadr, son of the martyred leader. He planned to institute sharia, a legal system based strictly on the Qur'an, and warned that if the Americans tried to interfere with the establishment of Shiite-dominated self-government, they would have to fight the whole Shiite population.

American leadership and public opinion reacted to the half-war, half-peace situation with a wide variety of responses. For critics of the war, the rising number of casualties, combined with the fact that no WMDs had yet been located in the country, was further evidence that the decision to go to war was flawed. Criticism of the administration of George W. Bush mounted. The criticism often took on a bitter tone, suggesting the president had betrayed the trust of the American people or that he had intentionally deceived the public and Congress regarding the level of domestic opposition to Hussein and the presence of WMDs.

Just as the war officially ended, Secretary of Defense Rumsfeld warned Syria not to provide aid to the resistance in Iraq or to help hide WMDs smuggled out of the country. Rumors persisted that the rail line to Syria from Iraq had carried several sealed carloads that may have

As the fighting wound down, many Iraqis fell victim to sabotage attacks. This youth awaits treatment from U.S. Army medics for burns suffered after a blast at an arms dump on the outskirts of Baghdad. *(Yannis Behrakis, Reuters/Landov)*

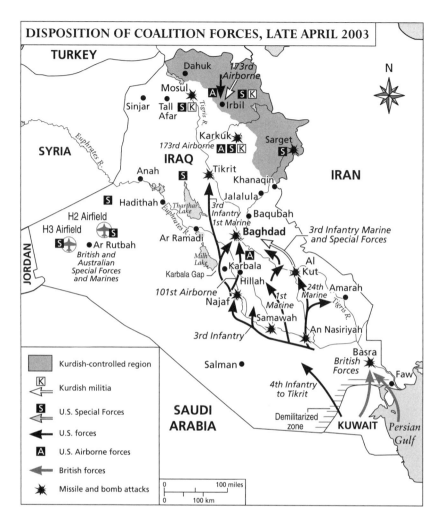

DISPOSITION OF COALITION FORCES, LATE APRIL 2003

contained chemicals, guarded by soldiers and Iraqi intelligence officials. By the first week in May, Syria responded by closing its border with Iraq and pledging to expel Iraqi officials who tried to take refuge there. President Bush said that Syria was "beginning to get the message." Rumors surfaced of a division between Secretary of State Powell and Rumsfeld over this issue and others, with Powell advocating a more diplomatic and less blunt warning to Syria. Despite such rumors, the administration continued to speak with one voice on the matter, reflecting an assurance

Syria and Iran
UNEASY NEIGHBORS

BY STUDYING THE MAP OF THE MIDDLE EAST AFTER THE Iraq War, it is easy to see how the Coalition defeat of Saddam Hussein's regime appeared to change the region's geopolitical balance—that is, the military and political allegiances of the bordering and nearby countries. In the post–Iraq War period, both countries had reason to feel uneasy about taking too strong an anti-American stand. The leaders of Syria and Iran began to withdraw financial and strategic support for anti-Israeli terrorist groups, and both countries gave signs that they were less anti-American than they had been in the past.

Syria was in a new situation. To the north of Syria lies Turkey, long an ally of the United States in the North Atlantic Treaty Organization (NATO). A major U.S. air base is located at Incirlik, less than 100 miles from the Syrian border. Early in the Iraq War, U.S. troops took over major airbases in the western Iraqi desert, near the eastern border of Syria. To the south of Syria lies Israel, still occupying the Golan Heights, a section of Syria about 30 miles from the Syrian capital, Damascus. Although not a formal military ally of the United States, Israel has many ties to the United States, which represent a continuing cause of concern to all the Arab nations.

Iran also found itself in a very different situation than that which had existed in summer 2002. By mid-2003, there were U.S. and NATO troops to the east of Iran in Afghanistan, and U.S. and British soldiers to the west of Iran in Iraq. Furthermore, although Washington promised to remove troops from Saudi Arabia, the United States Central Command was building a large base in the country of Qatar, directly across the Persian Gulf from Iran. Although the future was unclear, it seemed certain that in May 2003, the balance of military power in the region had shifted.

that the balance of power in the whole region had changed with the Coalition's defeat of the Iraqi regime, especially when coupled with the earlier defeat of the Taliban regime in Afghanistan.

Nevertheless, the border with Syria was "porous," with such a long length of it being desert that smugglers and refugees routinely crossed without passports. In Iraq, those living near the border often sent individuals across to Syria on errands to buy and bring back goods that were scarce and overpriced in Iraq.

Even for those who supported the war, the continuing casualty rate was disturbing. Some believed it could be addressed by sending a higher number of troops to Iraq. Others recommended rapid development of Iraqi police forces and even an Iraqi army that could assist in more stringent policing, particularly of the Sunni Triangle, where most of the casualties occurred.

Experts debated a number of overlapping issues. Since Hussein had not been captured or killed, and since statements from him were broadcast over radio from time to time, it appeared that the irregular activities were centrally coordinated by Hussein and remnants of the regime. However, it was not at all certain that Hussein remained in Iraq, and he might have taken refuge in a neighboring country, from which his taped statements were smuggled out for broadcast.

By late summer 2003, some analysts concluded that the level of resistance to the occupying forces was at least partially due to the infiltration into Iraq of anti-American Islamic fundamentalists, some of them linked to the al-Qaeda network. Such an observation was viewed differently depending on the slant or perspective of the analyst or editorialist. Those opposing the war and the Bush administration believed that any presence of al-Qaeda terrorists in postwar Iraq demonstrated that the war, instead of diminishing the threat to the United States from al-Qaeda, only increased it. On the other hand, supporters of the war argued that infiltration into Iraq of terrorists linked to al-Qaeda served to demonstrate the validity of the war, as part of the more general war on terror launched in response to the 9/11 attacks on the United States.

The occupying troops were caught in a classic dilemma. If they increased the application of force in attempts to establish order, they ran the risk of alienating the population. But if they did not conduct search-and-arrest missions and make a constant show of force, the insurgent resistance would only increase. An example of the problem came when U.S. troops searched the house of Fawzi Shafi, the editor of a weekly newspaper in Al Fallujah. Shafi had initially been a supporter of the Coalition and had not approved of Hussein; however, when U.S. troops in Operation Spartan Scorpion entered his house and forced him to the ground during their search, he felt abused. The troops confiscated his weapons. A few days later, when thugs burst into his neighboring brother's house, the householders had no weapons to protect themselves.

U.S. troops on police duty have the awkward choice of being too tough and alienating the civilian population or being too lenient and risking increased attacks from insurgents. Here, a civilian warily carries his daughter past heavily armed marines. *(Stefano Rellandini, Reuters/Landov)*

The thieves took the family's money and television set and walked off. Shafi and others like him believed they should be allowed to keep weapons for self-defense, especially in times of disruption and crime. Commentators feared that Coalition support among people like Shafi and his brother would quickly erode unless stability could be restored quickly.

The problems of the occupation forces were compounded by the spread of rumors and disinformation. Near Ar Ramadi, another town in the Sunni Triangle, Sheikh Khaled Saleh, a local businessman, imam, and outspoken critic of U.S. forces, told interviewers that the American officers had encouraged the looting and lawlessness, in order to have an "extra reason not to leave." He, like Shafi in Al Fallujah, complained that the confiscation of weapons left warehouses, supply facilities, stores, and homes unprotected.

The occupying forces were in a no-win situation. Sheikh Khaled complained that after confiscating the weapons, U.S. officers had promised more patrols by their troops to enforce order, and he claimed the patrols were too few because the soldiers were afraid of being shot. Yet when the patrols and raids were increased and weapons confiscated, the same Iraqis criticized the troops for excessive use of force.

The problems of the early occupation inevitably invoked comparisons with other countries that had been occupied and where "nation building" had taken place under U.S., Allied, or UN auspices. Two examples were held out by way of contrast. In Germany and Japan, after World War II, occupying forces had stayed for a decade, with military bases established and still in place 50 years later. After initial lawlessness in Germany, with some 40 occupying troops killed in the first two years, the country settled into the process of de-Nazification and rebuilding, emerging as a democracy with a democratically elected government in 1955. Japan's transition was even more orderly, with a complete revamping of the school system, elevation of the status of women, and the installation of a democratic regime in about the same period. But the contrast between these two nations and the situation in Iraq was striking.

Recruits to a new Iraqi police force sit in a classroom from which the window was torn during looting. *(Aladin Abdel Naby, Reuters/Landov)*

Both Germany and Japan were ethnically homogeneous countries; that is, neither country had large ethnic minorities. By contrast, Iraq was divided among Kurds, Turkomen, and Arabs, with the Arabs severely divided between Sunni and Shiite. Neither Germany nor Japan had a religiously inspired resistance. In Germany, Hitler had been killed at the end of the war; in Japan, Emperor Hirohito asked his followers to submit to surrender peacefully. In Iraq, Hussein continued to advocate resistance.

Nation building in other countries, however, had less success than in Germany and Japan. In Somalia and Haiti, after a brief stay in 1993 and 1994, U.S. troops pulled out, leaving behind chaotic and turbulent situations. In the former Yugoslavia, in the republic of Bosnia from 1992 and the Kosovo province of Serbia from 1998, NATO troops stayed on to maintain order for years after the conflict ended. Neither country became a fully functioning democracy, yet some order had been established. Furthermore, in Germany, Japan, Kosovo, and Bosnia, billions of dollars of foreign aid poured into the countries to help rebuild them. All of these experiences demonstrated that nation building took time, money, and patience.

Observers, both pro- and anti-war, questioned whether the Bush administration had developed a plan to rebuild and to "de-Baathize" Iraq in order to create a modern, democratic state with the needed legal and administrative structures. Those familiar with the process of nation building in other countries recognized that it would be an expensive and long-term process. By fall 2003, there were signs that while the fight to establish order and reduce casualties proceeded, Coalition authorities were beginning to face the deeper issue of how to rebuild and establish a permanent democratic government.

13
AFTERMATH

The efforts to track down and capture or kill the key personnel of the Hussein regime continued through summer 2003, with mixed success. On July 22, U.S. troops in the northern city of Mosul followed up on a tip and surrounded what ended up being the hideout of Uday and Qusay Hussein, the sons of Saddam Hussein. After

Pictured here with their father are Uday (left) and Qusay Hussein (right). Both sons were killed in a fierce firefight on July 22, 2003. *(Reuters/Landov)*

Delegates to an early conference of the Iraqi interim Governing Council applaud a series of compromises. The authority formed the basis for a temporary government in 2003–04. *(Senior Airman Tammy L. Grider, Department of Defense)*

a six-hour firefight in which four Coalition troops were wounded, the two brothers were killed. In an effort to convince the Iraqi public that they had really died in the fight, gruesome pictures of their dead bodies were released to the press. U.S. army general Ricardo Sanchez announced the killing and suggested that their death might reduce the support for the Hussein regime. Nonetheless, the number of attacks on U.S., British, and other forces occupying Iraq continued to mount in late summer and early fall 2003.

Gradually, the outline of a plan for transition to local control emerged. In August, the United States began training and graduating members of a new Iraqi Civil Defense Corps that would serve in a police role and eventually expand to form an army that could be used to restore and preserve order. Recruits to the force were paid $120 a month, about twice the salary of former soldiers of the Iraqi army. The Governing Council, consisting of 25 Iraqi political leaders selected by the Coalition, began regularly meeting and taking control of some government functions. By

October, the council announced plans to hold an election for a constitutional assembly, with a schedule to establish the new constitution by mid-2004. As the Governing Council began to exercise its authority, it, like the occupying forces, found itself in a difficult position. If it took strong actions against Hussein supporters, it would be criticized for taking an undemocratic stand. If it did not take action, it would be criticized for its weakness.

Closure of al-Arabiya

IN NOVEMBER 2003, THE IRAQI GOVERNING COUNCIL ordered the closure of the Baghdad office of Arabic-language satellite television network, al-Arabiya, and sent representatives from the council-controlled Information Ministry to seize the network's satellite linkage equipment. The action was taken because the network had broadcast an audiotape of a speech by Saddam Hussein that called on Iraqis to resist the occupation and to elect new officials, not from among the council but from among representatives of the former regime.

The news director of al-Arabiya, Salah Negm, denied that the station had been inciting violence by airing the tape. Rather, he claimed, such a broadcast represented an effort to report the facts to the public. That Hussein was alive and still making appeals to the Iraqi people was news, and reporting the news represented a key element of a free press and a democratic state. In fact, the tape had been broadcast from the Dubai headquarters of the network, but it was the Baghdad bureau of al-Arabiya that was closed.

The Governing Council claimed that it was no infringement on freedom of the press to shut down the local office of a television network that openly broadcasts an incitement to acts of violence. At the same time, Jalal Talabani, a member of the Governing Council, announced that the council would retain the right to close down any media outlet, even the British Broadcasting Corporation, if the council believed the facility was guilty of incitement.

It was a classic case of freedom of the press. Can a democracy exist that allows the freedom of critics to ask for its own destruction? Can a democracy exist that denies the freedom of critics to say what they believe? The resolution, in this case at least, would be a temporary closing of al-Arabiya that would serve as a warning to others.

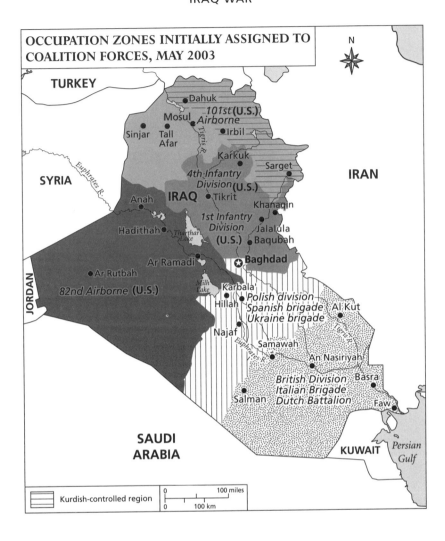

OCCUPATION ZONES INITIALLY ASSIGNED TO
COALITION FORCES, MAY 2003

N

TURKEY

Dahuk

101st (U.S.)
Airborne

Mosul

Sinjar   Tall
Afar

Irbil

Karkuk

Sarget

IRAN

SYRIA

4th Infantry
Division (U.S.)

IRAQ   Tikrit

Khanaqin

Anah

1st Infantry
Division   Jalalula

Hadithah   Tharthar
Lake

(U.S.)   Baqubah

Ar Ramadi   Baghdad

JORDAN

Ar Rutbah

82nd Airborne (U.S.)

Milh
Lake

Karbala

Hillah   Polish division
Spanish brigade   Al Kut
Ukraine brigade

Najaf

Samawah

An Nasiriyah

British Division   Basra
Italian Brigade
Salman   Dutch Battalion   Faw

SAUDI
ARABIA

KUWAIT   Persian
Gulf

Kurdish-controlled region   0   100 miles
                             0   100 km

By November 2003, the polls in the United States indicated that public support for the policy of the Bush administration in Iraq had diminished. Earlier, in March and April, when the war was being fought, polling had regularly shown more than 70 percent in favor of the president's conduct of the war, despite intense criticism and doubts raised in the media. By November, the support for the president's policy toward Iraq hovered around 50 percent. Nevertheless, it seemed that the American public had come to accept a continuing presence of U.S. troops in Iraq. Despite the frequent reports of new casualties there from shootings, mines, and suicide bombs, it was apparent that the administration and the public were reconciled to a long and difficult endgame.

By November, the total number of U.S. troops killed in Iraq had climbed above 400, including the 115 before May 1. Attacks were not directed only at Americans. The British reported a total of 52 deaths in Iraq, and 16 Italian police officers had been killed in a single attack. In addition, Denmark, Poland, Spain, and the Ukraine had each suffered the death of one soldier. Some observers believed that the insurgents in Iraq especially targeted international organizations and troops of other nations in order to increase the pressure to end the occupation. In the face of what a representative called an "extremely dangerous and volatile situation" in Iraq, the International Committee of the Red Cross ended its operations in Iraq after a detonation of a car bomb outside its offices on October 27, 2003, which killed 12 people.

In the United States and Britain, critics of the original decision to go to war voiced objections, some old, some new. In books and articles, on the Internet, and on call-in talk radio and television some of the lines of criticism focused on perceived distortions, disinformation, or outright lies. Some critics charged that President Bush and Prime Minister Blair had intentionally slanted or misused information gathered by intelligence agencies to exaggerate or even invent the evidence that the Hussein regime had a program of WMDs. Such criticism was based on the logic that if the search teams in Iraq discovered no weapons, then the evidence for their existence must have been distorted or invented. Defenders of the U.S. president and British prime minister pointed out that there were many other explanations that fit the historical evidence.

It was possible that Hussein and his regime had wanted to deny officially the existence of WMDs to the United Nations but leave neighboring countries, such as Kuwait, Saudi Arabia, Qatar, and Iran, with the impression that the weapons were still there. Hans Blix, who had headed both UNSCOM and UNMOVIC, suggested that it was quite possible that all or almost all of the WMD programs had been ended but that Hussein wanted to leave the sense of doubt in neighboring states so that his regime would appear more powerful than it was. Furthermore, Hussein's stance of defiance of the United Nations and its resolutions may have been intended not to conceal existing weapons but to enhance his reputation as a powerful and threatening leader of a well-armed state.

Other explanations were less subtle. Some simply believed that WMD supplies, particularly poison gas, had been very carefully hidden and that the documentation for their production and storage was also well hidden. Rumors of secret shipments of whole railcar loads of concealed cargo to Syria led some to believe that the weapons had been simply packed up and sent out during the war.

Critics were even more disturbed at another justification for the war: that Hussein's regime had supported terrorists. There was, in fact, no direct evidence that the Hussein regime had supported, with funds, arms, or intelligence, al-Qaeda terrorists. Although President Bush had never directly asserted that Hussein and al-Qaeda were closely linked, he had many times stated that the Iraq government was a supporter of terrorism, without specifying which terrorists or on what evidence he was basing the charge. Although the Iraqi regime had maintained terrorist training camps and an al-Qaeda-related training facility had operated in a remote corner of the Kurdish zone, no direct al-Qaeda linkage to Hussein was ever established by the end of 2003. Even so, polls indicated that a majority of the American public believed Hussein had supported al-Qaeda. Some critics of President Bush believed he had intentionally planted that impression to support a war.

When critics sought to explain what might have motivated the president and his advisers to intentionally start a war with what they charged was so little real justification, a range of answers were provided. Some alleged he was motivated by an attempt to complete the war that his father, George H. W. Bush, had begun, the Persian Gulf War of 1991. Others saw even more sinister motives, such as seeking control of Iraqi oil. Some simply believed that Bush and Blair were power crazed or unsophisticated, or both.

Although the media, including published books and Internet sources, were full of such charges and assertions, the general public and Congress appeared willing to see the difficult occupation through to some kind of peaceful resolution. Exactly how long it would take, how much it would cost in dollars and in lives, and whether the resulting state would be a fair and democratic one, all remained to be seen.

However, 2004 would be a presidential election year in the United States. In several prior wars in which the United States participated, the nature of the war and the disengagement of American forces overseas had become a political issue during a presidential election year. In 1952, the Republican Dwight Eisenhower successfully campaigned against the record of the administration of Harry Truman in the Korean War. In a similar way, Richard Nixon won the election of 1968 and began the long and difficult process of extracting American troops from Vietnam in a war that had been started under the prior administration of Lyndon Johnson. Political observers speculated whether the Democratic Party would put forward a candidate for the presidency in 2004 who would tap into a similar discontent with the engagement of American forces overseas.

More important for the people of Iraq was the nature of conditions there. As winter approached, it was not exactly clear whether the continued insurgency was based on wide popular support by Iraqis. The French media had begun to call the insurgent forces and their actions the "resistance," seemingly sympathizing with the action and invoking memories of their own resistance to the German occupation in World War II. However, the degree of Iraqi support for the acts of violence against American, British, and other occupying forces was difficult to measure, and it appeared that most Iraqis simply waited to see how things would turn out, rather than actively supporting the insurgency. Increasingly, Coalition commanders on the ground had come to believe that the insurgents were a mix of "foreign fighters," some from al-Qaeda, some from Iran, with local thugs who were paid by former Baath regime

Through late 2003 and early 2004, Iraqis continued to protest the presence of Coalition troops. *(Sergeant Albert Eaddy, Department of Defense)*

officials to commit individual acts. As arrests and raids by U.S. troops in the Sunni Triangle continued, more and more information that supported this view was collected.

Meanwhile, the U.S. Congress had approved appropriation of $18.6 billion for the reconstruction of Iraq, to be spent on communications, infrastructure, power supply, and training. In early December, former secretary of state James Baker was sent on a special mission to Russia, Germany, France, and other countries, asking them to write off or cancel debts owed by Iraq to them as a form of aid that would reduce the burden on Iraq. At the same time as Baker was making his rounds, the Defense Department announced that the 26 prime contracts for reconstruction of Iraq would only be issued to companies in countries that had supported the Coalition.

Reaction to these contracting restrictions among non-Coalition countries was one of shock. Foreign leaders and some editorial writers in the United States criticized the Bush administration for such open use of pressure and threat. A spokesperson for the French foreign ministry stated that the French government would study the legality of the decision; the German government claimed the decision was "unacceptable" and not in the spirit of international cooperation and looking forward, rather than backward at prior lack of support for U.S. and British policy. However, a White House spokesperson announced that money provided by U.S. taxpayers should go directly to the Iraqi people and to those countries that had worked with the United States in trying to build a free Iraq. Within days, both France and Germany agreed to partially reduce the debts owed their nations as a result of the requests made by Baker on his mission, soon followed by similar reductions in debt owed to other nations.

At the same time as the international community debated the question of how the money to rebuild Iraq would be spent, the raids and arrests by Coalition forces in Iraq began to zero in on the "outer circle" of supporters and friends of Hussein. Gradually, the military improved its work as a police and detective force. By early December 2003, interrogation of prisoners captured in such raids led to the inner circle of associates who had helped conceal Hussein since the end of the fighting.

On December 13, at about 8:30 P.M., local time, a unit of 600 U.S. troops from the 4th Infantry Division raided a farmhouse in the small town of Adwar, just south of Tikrit, and captured Saddam Hussein, who was found hiding in a small hole in the ground there. Although he had a pistol with him, he was captured without a fight. Throughout Iraq, spontaneous celebrations broke out as the news spread. Perhaps to emphasize the defeated and humbled state of Hussein, pictures showing him with several months' growth of hair and beard, being examined by a military doctor, were broadcast and published around the world.

Saddam Hussein was captured December 13, 2003, and pictures showing his disheveled appearance were released around the world. *(Department of Defense)*

148

IRAQIRAQ WAR

News announcements from Paul Bremer, the U.S. representative in Iraq, from the Iraqi Governing Council, and from President Bush all took the same tone: The capture of Hussein would represent a chance for the Iraqi people to put an era behind them and to move forward to rebuild their society. The Governing Council had just enacted a law establishing a special civil court for the trial of war criminals and those accused of crimes against humanity, and the council fully expected that the trial of Hussein before that court would be conducted in a manner consistent with international standards of justice. In January 2004, U.S. authorities announced that Hussein's status was that of a prisoner of war, which would allow him either to be tried by the United States or turned over to the Iraqi authorities for trial.

The question that faced Iraq and the world community at the beginning of 2004 was whether the capture of Hussein and most of the high-ranking members of his former regime would bring a decrease in the armed insurgency. In fact, the insurgency only increased after his arrest. Families of U.S., British, Polish, Spanish, Italian, and Ukrainian servicepeople in the occupation of Iraq discovered that his peacefeul surrender did not end the violent phase of the aftermath of the Iraq War of 2003. When terrorists detonated bombs aboard a commuter train in Madrid, Spain, on March 11, 2004, the Spanish people reacted by voting out their conservative government. The new Socialist prime minister, José Luis Rodríguez Zapatero, ordered the evacuation of Spanish troops from Iraq on July 1.

In 2004, the casualty rate among American and other Coalition forces serving in Iraq continued to climb. The number of deaths of U.S. troops went above 700 by the time of the handover of sovereignty from Ambassador Paul Bremer, U.S civil administrator, to the Iraqi interim government. That handover, scheduled for June 30, 2004, took place in a quiet ceremony two days early on Monday, June 28, partly to forestall the timing of any further terrorist actions scheduled to disrupt the process. Within days, the new Iraqi prime minister, Iyad Alawai, stated that he intended to take a firm line, using emergency powers to arrest insurgents. Even so, American casualties surpassed the 1,000 mark by September 8.

During the first half of 2004, as the American public awaited the handover and prepared for the upcoming presidential elections in the United States in November, opinion over the war divided even more sharply. Some leading Democrats charged President Bush with incompetence, lack of judgment, and inexperience and with alienating U.S.

AFTERMATH

Ambassador Paul Bremer (left) and Iraqi president Sheikh Ghazi Ajil as-Yawar shake hands during the ceremony in Baghdad in which full governmental authority was transferred to the Iraq interim government on June 28, 2004. *(Staff Sergeant D. Myles Cullen, Department of Defense)*

allies around the world by the invasion of Iraq and its troubled aftermath. Defenders of the president and his policies continued to charge his critics with distortion for political gain.

Controversies swirled around many separate issues. Former State Department official Joseph Wilson revealed that he had investigated whether the African country of Niger had supplied uranium to Iraq and that his report indicating there had been no such contacts had been available to President Bush by early 2003. The president had mentioned the Niger-Iraq connection in his speech asking support from Congress for the ultimatum and invasion of Iraq, apparently ignoring Wilson's report, if he had seen it. Defenders of the president pointed out that Wilson's report had been based on discussions at a hotel swimming pool in Niger and that those conversations hardly constituted a real investigation. Then, conservative journalist Robert Novak revealed that Wilson's wife was an analyst at the CIA. Wilson immediately charged that Novak had ruined her career by revealing her secret position. The tempest over this issue continued, as Wilson's critics explained that the position his

wife held was no secret, that she was
not an agent but simply an analyst,
and that revealing her job was not a
criminal act.

Another scandal surrounded the
revelation that Iraqi prisoners held
in the Abu Ghraib prison in Iraq by
U.S. forces had been subjected to
humiliating treatment by guards. The
treatment included being stripped
naked and threatened with dogs.
Male prisoners had been photographed in the nude in the presence
of mocking female U.S. enlisted personnel. Prisoners had been threatened with electric shock and had
been chained in restraint. More
seriously, a number of prisoners
had died in captivity, in some cases,
their relatives claimed, because of
neglect, beatings, or other mistreatment. The charges circulated quietly
for several months and were under
investigation by the military. When
several compact discs of pictures of
the practices were leaked to the press,
the televised and published images
made the issue even more shocking.

In the United States, officials
made explicit apologies for the pris-
oners' treatment and conducted investigations, attempting to discover
who was to blame. Critics suggested that the precedent of considering the
detainees held in Guantánamo not as prisoners of war but as enemy combatants had set the tone for mistreatment of prisoners in Iraq. Others
claimed that the fault lay with zealous contractors who had been hired to
serve at the prison or that the blame could be placed on a limited number of enlisted personnel who simply abused their power. The fact that
many of the treatments seemed designed to exploit aspects of Arab and
Muslim culture suggested to many that the practices were not a local

On May 24, 2004, Coalition forces in Baghdad secure a car-bombing scene near the entrance to the Coalition Provisional Authority headquarters. *(Technical Sergeant Roy Santana, Department of Defense)*

mistake but reflected an intelligence technique that relied on violating a prisoner's cultural norms without inflicting physical harm. Such a sophisticated mental torture method was probably not developed by enlisted personnel with little training in interrogation, observers noted.

Many critics of the war in both Britain and the United States charged that one original casus belli, the charge that Hussein had weapons of mass destruction, had been proven false by the failure to find any such weapons. The flawed intelligence, the critics charged, did not arise from a simple mistake or misreading of data. The harshest critics of the war argued that President Bush and his advisers had decided to go to war against Iraq and had sought some justification for doing so. Faced with that decision, intelligence analysts misinterpreted their information out of a concern to provide the administration with the information they knew was wanted and needed. Such a distortion could have been unconscious, a form of "group-think" that led to the charges that Saddam Hussein's government was armed with poison gas, biological weapons, and possibly radiological dirty bombs, as well as long-range missiles to deliver such means of mass destruction. The implication for the president's opponents seemed clear. He had either intentionally or unintentionally distorted the evidence to convince others to support his war plan, they argued. If he had done so intentionally, his actions were reprehensible; if he had done so unintentionally, his actions reflected incompetence.

Such comments, of course, ignored the fact that international inspectors under both the UNSCOM and UNMOVIC organizations had encountered repeated noncooperation on the part of Hussein's government. Whether there really had been such weapons there, Hussein's defiance of the UN inspection system was very well documented. As Hans Blix had noted, even if Hussein had no WMDs, he certainly behaved as if he had them, and it would have taken the inspectors much longer to satisfy themselves and the world community that there were no such weapons programs in operation in Iraq.

Yet another scandal surfaced over the UN-sponsored Oil-for-Food program. Under that system, UN officials had allowed a limited quantity of Iraqi oil to be sold on the international market. The reason was that the funds could be used to provide aid to the Iraqi people in the form of food, medicine, and health care that would be in scarce supply because of the sanctions imposed against the Hussein regime. Investigations in early 2004 revealed that highly placed opponents in the United Kingdom and in France of British prime minister Tony Blair and U.S. president Bush had appeared to receive funds siphoned off from the project. Furthermore, funds that were supposed to be channeled to relief in the Kurdish part of Iraq simply did not get passed through the UN agencies at all. Sunni Arabs who shared Hussein's animosity to the Kurds administered some of those agencies. Other funds produced by the oil transactions apparently were available to Hussein for supporting his personal lifestyle and for armaments.

During all of these debates that kept journalists and television talk-show hosts busy following up leads and investigating the stories, many of the American and other Coalition troops in Iraq complained that no one was reporting the "good" news. News media conventionally report events that are shocking, immoral, or tragic, but the officers and troops in Iraq wondered why no one back home heard about the success stories. Journalists apparently did not think it was very newsworthy that throughout Iraq electric power was being restored, people were driving their cars to work, buying cell phones, reading more newspapers, listening to a variety of television channels, and freely discussing politics. Universities and schools were opened and well attended. Damaged hospitals and clinics had been repaired and took in patients, and food and all sorts of consumer goods appeared in the marketplaces. Despite the car bombs, remotely detonated roadside explosives, and the sniper attacks, there was lots of very ordinary life going on. The ordinary was not news, even if the soldiers and marines on the ground felt that it should be.

Out of the glare of publicity, U.S. troops conducted a very wide variety of duties that ranged well beyond the highly publicized efforts to ensure security and stability. American soldiers and marines trained Iraqi police personnel, set up hospitals and provided health services,

During advance military training conducted by the U.S. Army, Iraqi soldiers practice urban war-fighting techniques. *(Staff Sergeant Myles D. Cullen, Department of Defense)*

cleared mines, and helped arrange local elections. As American troops and contractors repaired roads, bridges, refineries, water supply systems, and power plants, such practical work simply received little notice.

With the handover of sovereignty to the interim Iraqi government, the situation changed rather abruptly. The causes of the war and the difficult conduct of the transfer of authority remained politically debated issues in the United States. Nevertheless, it was clear that the United States intended to withdraw from the country and to leave the resolution of the internal politics and the establishment of a stable regime in the hands of the Iraqis. Even though critics had charged that the sovereignty transfer would be artificial and that the United States would still be making the crucial decisions, the new regime made a clear effort to exert its own authority. A timetable of elections through 2005 and 2006 showed the pathway to full Iraqi self-government.

The war itself became one of the issues in the U.S. presidential election of 2004. President Bush defended the decision to go to war, continuing to assert that the defeat of Saddam Hussein represented the beginnings of democracy for Iraq and a step in the War on Terrorism. Democratic Party candidate for the presidency Senator John Kerry of Massachusetts argued that the Iraq War had been the wrong war and that it had been conducted wrongly. He insisted that in the future, the United States should be careful to work with its allies and that, as president, he would seek to establish a clear strategy to remove American troops from Iraq.

The Iraq War, which had been fought so quickly and decisively in the period from March 19, 2003, to May 1, 2003, had led to a military occupation that was drawn out into one of the most divisive and hotly debated international events in U.S. history by late 2004. Whether Americans would be able to discuss the issues with civility and with information, rather than with name-calling and bitterness, would be the real test of American democracy in the months and years to come.

Glossary

air campaign Attack without any troops on the ground, using land- and sea-based aircraft and missiles launched from land, air, or sea.

antimissile missile A missile intended as a defensive weapon to destroy incoming missiles. In the Iraq War, the United States used the anti-aircraft Patriot missile as an antimissile missile.

antipersonnel weapon Weapon designed to kill troops rather than destroy equipment.

asymmetrical warfare Warfare conducted by alternate means, such as guerrilla or terrorist attacks, in which one side has much smaller forces, not symmetrical in strength with the other side, but nevertheless presenting challenges conventional forces find difficult to counter.

AWACS (airborne warning and control system) A large aircraft designed to provide radar and communications backup to fighter and bomber aircraft.

attack positions Preassigned rest points established for advancing U.S. troops to stop, rest, and refuel during the Iraq War.

barrel A unit of measurement for crude oil, equal to 42 U.S. gallons.

black market A system for the sale of illicit goods, such as stolen property, drugs, or currency at an unofficial rate of exchange.

Bradley A U.S. Army infantry fighting vehicle, tanklike in appearance, with tracks and armor; it has a crew of three and can carry six infantry into battle. It is named after World War II general Omar Bradley, the "GI General."

bunker A concrete shelter against missile or bomb attacks, usually underground.

cache A hidden stockpile or collection, as of weapons or ammunition.

calutron A device for the separation of uranium-235 from uranium-238 using electromagnets.

cartel An organization designed to control prices for a product. The Organization of Petroleum Exporting Countries (OPEC) is a cartel made up of the oil ministers of some of the world's leading oil-producing nations.

casualties Members of the military killed, wounded, or taken prisoner in a battle or war.

casus belli From the Latin for "occasion for war" (sometimes incorrectly spelled *causus belli*), in international law it refers to a hostile act, an invasion, or an act of state-supported terrorism or sabotage against another nation.

chemical weapons Various forms of poison gas, including nerve gas, chlorine, and phosgene. Chemical weapons have rarely been used in warfare since World War I, but Iraq used them in its 1980–88 war with Iran and against Iraqi Kurds in the town of Halabja in 1988.

Coalition The 2003 alliance that opposed the Iraqi regime, consisting of the United States, Great Britain, Australia, Poland, and the Czech Republic. Although another 25 or so nations supported the action, they did not provide armed forces. The alliance against Iraq in the 1991 Persian Gulf War was also called the Coalition.

collateral damage Unintended human casualties and/or property damage beyond the intended specific target.

commando Highly trained forces used for special operations, such as landing behind enemy lines to destroy key facilities. The U.S. Navy Seals, the U.S. Army Rangers, and the British Special Armed Service (SAS) are commando units.

conventions of war The guidelines for conduct of war and the humane treatment of prisoners, as defined in several treaties signed by multiple countries and the rules developed by nations to implement the guidelines.

crude oil Petroleum, before being refined into gasoline and other products.

cruise missile A missile designed to fly at a relatively low level at extremely high speed, guided to its target by an internal computer. Cruise missiles can be ship-launched, ground-launched, or air-launched.

demolition   The act of a retreating force's destroying, usually by explosives, resources that might be of use to the enemy, such as a bridge, warehouse, or fortification.

drone aircraft   A pilotless aircraft used to conduct aerial photography or to drop weapons over enemy positions.

embedded reporters   Press and electronic media reporters and photographers who traveled closely with units of troops in Operation Iraqi Freedom to report conditions and actions directly from the front. Such reporters agreed not to report any specific information that would place their associated troops in increased danger.

fascism   A system of government historically associated with Benito Mussolini's Italy and characterized by a dictator, centralized controls of the economy and society, suppression of most opposition, and often involving appeals to nationalism.

feint   A false move, intended to convince the enemy that an advance is about to occur in one area to draw attention away from a genuine attack in another area.

flank   In military jargon, the sides of a military position. The left flank of the enemy position describes the side to the left from the viewpoint of the attacker. As a verb, to flank or outflank is to move so as to attack on the side.

fog of war   The confusion that arises from lack of information, rapid response, and high-risk action during battle.

gulf states   The Persian Gulf States of Kuwait, Qatar, Bahrain, United Arab Emirates, and Oman.

Humvee   A light, all-terrain vehicle, larger and more rugged than the traditional jeep. Its name is a contraction of HMMWV, which stands for high-mobility multipurpose wheeled vehicle.

infrastructure   The network of communication, utility, and transportation facilities of a nation, including electric utilities, telephone networks, radio and television stations, water supply and sewage, highways, bridges, railroads, and airports.

irregulars   Military fighters who do not wear uniforms and who usually operate in small bands independently of each other.

al-Jazeera   An independent Arabic television news channel based in Qatar, known for its criticism of some Arab regimes, as well as U.S. and European policies.

jus ad bellum Latin for "justification of war," it refers to the several lines of argument that make a war a proper action under the "just war" concept originally developed by the 13th-century philosopher Thomas Aquinas.

laser guided Of a bomb or missile equipped with a seeker device and movable fins so that it can home in on the reflection of a laser beam aimed at a target.

logistics The military science of organizing and transporting supplies and equipment needed for battle.

looting The act of openly stealing private or public property during a time of civil disruption when police presence is diminished.

mechanized infantry Troops who mostly fight on foot but are transported by vehicles and are supported by light armored vehicles, such as tanks and personnel carriers.

militiamen Usually untrained civilians who participate as fighters on a part-time basis during a time of conflict. In Iraq, they were often based on units of the Baath Party.

mobile launcher Transport-erector-launchers (TELs) for missiles so that they can be moved from place to place. Scuds mounted on TELs allow quick removal so that retaliatory strikes do not destroy the crew.

MRE Meal-ready-to-eat, the standard ration provided to U.S. troops in the field.

net importer A nation that imports more of a certain product or commodity than it exports, such as when the United States began to import more petroleum than it sold overseas by the 1950s.

nuclear proliferation The spread or proliferation of nuclear weapons to countries other than the original five nations that developed them in the period 1945–64 (United States, Soviet Union, Britain, France, and China).

On-Site Inspection Agency (OSIA) A U.S. military organization established to verify arms agreements with the Soviet Union by observing the destruction of nuclear weapons and delivery systems; provided staff help to UNSCOM inspectors.

pan-Arabism The concept of the unity of Arabic-speaking peoples, who live in more than 15 nations in the region from Morocco in Northwest Africa to Iraq in south-central Asia.

pincer movement An advance on an enemy position from two directions, like the closing of a pincer or pair of pliers.

preemption Taking an action in order to prevent another's action. A preemptive war is one that is fought to prevent the attacked country from attacking first. The United States had rarely engaged in preemptive war prior to the attack on Iraq.

propaganda Originally any information released, or "propagated," the term refers to slanted or manufactured information designed by a government or political group to sway opinion.

al-Qaeda Literally translated from Arabic as "the base." The loose organization of terrorists funded by fundamentalist Muslims and coordinated by Osama bin Laden and a group of associates who were based in Afghanistan in the year 2001.

Qur'an (Koran) The holy book of the Muslim religion, consisting of the collected sayings and wisdom of the Prophet Muhammad (A.D. 570–632).

Ramadan In the Muslim calendar, the ninth month of the year, regarded as a holy period for prayer, reading the Qur'an, and daytime fasting. In 1991, Ramadan officially began on March 17. In 2003, Ramadan began in November.

refugees People fleeing from war zones or political, ethnic, or religious oppression.

scramble The takeoff of one or more aircraft for a sortie.

Scud Missiles constructed by Iraqis by welding together two SS-1 (surface-to-surface, type 1) missiles provided by the Soviet Union, reputedly increasing their range to more than 500 miles. In 1990, Iraq had an estimated 65 Scud missiles.

Security Council The body of the United Nations charged with deciding on matters of international security, made up of representatives of five permanent members and 10 rotating members. The permanent members can veto a measure, while the nonpermanent members can only vote for or against a measure. A single veto by a permanent member will prevent a Security Council resolution from passing. In 2003, the permanent members were the United States, United Kingdom, Russia, China, and France. The 10 rotating members were Bulgaria, Cameroon, Guinea, Mexico, and Syria, whose term ended in December 2003, and Angola, Chile, Germany, Pakistan, and Spain, with terms ending in December 2004.

IRAQ WAR

sharia The code of conduct of Muslims, rather more strictly enforced among the Shiite than among the Sunni Muslims. In some Muslim countries, it has become the basis of civil and criminal law.

Shiite One of the two major divisions of the Muslim religion, whose members tend to closely rely on the advice of religious leaders in matters of political, social, and moral concerns. The Shiites disagree with the Sunni branch of the religion over questions of the legitimate successors to Muhammad as well as over matters of adherence to the sharia.

slant The editorial bias or implied position in the treatment of events that appears in newspaper and television reporting of events.

sortie An individual aircraft flight, from takeoff through landing.

Sunni One of the two major branches of the Muslim religion that is less strict in adherence to the sharia. Saddam Hussein and many of his most loyal followers were Sunnis.

Sunni Triangle A term introduced in the media following the defeat of the Iraqi army, describing the region north of Baghdad in the triangle formed by that city, Tikrit in the north, and Ar Ramadi to the west; a majority of the inhabitants of this region are Sunni Arabs. The resistance to U.S. occupation forces appeared most severe here.

Taliban Literally, "students," a group of graduates of religious schools who established a strict, fundamentalist regime in Afghanistan in 1993. The regime provided haven for Osama bin Laden and members of the al-Qaeda organization in the period from 1999 to 2001.

technical A civilian vehicle, such as a pickup truck, on which a heavy machine gun or light artillery piece is mounted.

Tomahawk A sea-launched cruise missile, used by the U.S. Navy for the first time in warfare during the Persian Gulf War. The missile is guided by terrain contour.

veto The act of defeating a measure or resolution with a single opposing vote. In the UN Security Council, five permanent members each have the right to defeat a measure even if all the others support it.

Vietnam effect Following the Vietnam War, the American public resisted the use of U.S. troops overseas. American and foreign leaders believed the Vietnam effect would prevent any sustained use of U.S. military force in the case of Iraq in 2003.

ultimatum   A statement that unless a certain action is taken, severe consequences will follow at a defined date and time.

weapons of mass destruction (**WMDs**)   Weapons capable of killing many people at a time, including nuclear and thermonuclear bombs and missiles, radiological weapons that disperse radioactive materials by the detonation of a high-explosive device, poison gas, and biological weapons that spread disease.

Further Reading

NONFICTION

Albright, David. "Trouble in the Gulf." *Bulletin of the Atomic Scientists* (May/June 1998), pp. 44–50.

Albright, David, and Mark Hibbs. "Iraq's Nuclear Hide and Seek." *Bulletin of the Atomic Scientists* (September 1991), pp. 14–23.

Baker, James. *The Politics of Diplomacy: Revolution, War and Peace, 1989–1992.* New York: G. P. Putnam's Sons, 1995.

Bin, Alberto, Richard Hill, and Archer Jones. *Desert Storm: A Forgotten War.* Westport, Conn.: Praeger, 1998.

Bodansky, Yossef. *Bin Laden: The Man Who Declared War on America.* New York: Prima, 2001.

Burke, Jason. *Al Qaeda: Casting a Shadow of Terror.* New York: I. B. Taurus, 2003.

Bush, George H. W., and Brent Scowcroft. *A World Transformed.* New York: Alfred A. Knopf, 1998.

Bush, George W. *We Will Prevail.* New York: Continuum Press, 2003.

Carlisle, Rodney. *Complete Idiot's Guide to Spies and Espionage.* New York: Alpha Books, 2003.

———. *The Persian Gulf War.* New York: Facts On File, 2003.

Cockburn, Andrew, and Patrick Cockburn. *Out of the Ashes: The Resurrection of Saddam Hussein.* New York: HarperCollins Publishers, 1999.

Cordesman, Anthony. *The Iraq War: A Working Chronology.* Washington, D.C.: Center for Strategic and International Studies, 2003.

———. *The Iraq War: Strategy, Tactics, and Military Lessons.* Westport, Conn.: Praeger, 2003.

Clark, Wesley K. *Winning Modern Wars: Iraq, Terrorism, and the American Empire.* New York: Public Affairs, 2003.

Dickey, Christopher, and Donatella Lorch. "Iraq's Most Wanted." *Newsweek* (March 31, 2003), 49–53.

Freedman, Lawrence. *The Gulf Conflict, 1990–1991: Diplomacy and War in the New World Order.* Princeton, N.J.: Princeton University Press, 1993.

Friedrich, Otto, ed. *Desert Storm: The War in the Persian Gulf.* Boston: Little Brown, 1991.

Hamza, Khidhir. *Saddam's Bombmaker.* New York: Simon and Schuster, 2000.

Hiro, Dilip. *Holy Wars: The Rise of Islamic Fundamentalism.* New York: Routledge Press, 1989.

Hirsch, Michael. "The Aftermath: Bombs, then Building." *Newsweek* (March 31, 2003), 44–45.

Hoffmann, Bruce. *Inside Terrorism.* New York: Columbia University Press, 1998.

Kaplan, Lawrence F., and William Kristol. *The War over Iraq: Saddam's Tyranny and America's Mission.* San Francisco: Encounter Books, 2003.

Liu, Melinda. "Live from Baghdad." *Newsweek* (March 31, 2003), 32–38.

Makiya, Kanan. *Republic of Fear: The Politics of Modern Iraq.* Berkeley: University of California Press, 1998.

McGeary, Johanna. "Iraq after Saddam." *Time* (March 10, 2003), 28–33.

Miller, Judith, and Laurie Mylroie. *Saddam Hussein and the Crisis in the Gulf.* New York: Random House, 1990.

Moore, Robin. *The Hunt for Bin Laden: Task Force Dagger.* New York: Ballantine, 2003.

Morrison, David E. *Television and the Gulf War.* London: John Libbey, 1992.

Murray, Williamson, and Robert H. Scales, Jr. *The Iraq War: A Military History.* Cambridge, Mass.: Belknap Press of Harvard University, 2003.

Nye, Joseph S., Jr., and Roger K. Smith, eds. *After the Storm: Lessons from the Gulf War.* Lanham, Md.: Madison Books, 1992.

Pollack, Kenneth M. *The Threatening Storm.* New York: Random House, 2002.

Powell, Colin, with Joseph Persico. *My American Journey.* New York: Ballantine, 1995.

Ritter, Scott. *Endgame: Solving the Iraq Problem—Once and for All.* New York: Simon and Schuster, 1999.

Sasson, Jean P. *The Rape of Kuwait: The True Story of Iraqi Atrocities against a Civilian Population.* New York: Knightsbridge, 1991.

Scheer, Christopher, Robert Scheer, and Lakshmi Chaudry. *The Five Biggest Lies Bush Told Us about Iraq.* New York: Independent Media Institute, 2003.

Schulz, William. *Tainted Legacy: 9/11 and the Ruin of Human Rights.* New York: Thunder's Mouth Press, 2003.

Sifry, Micah, and Christopher Cerf. *The Gulf War Reader: History, Documents, Opinions.* New York: Times Books, 1991.

———. *The Iraq War Reader: History, Documents, Opinions.* New York: Times Books, 2003.

Timmerman, Kenneth. *The Death Lobby: How the West Armed Iraq.* New York: Houghton-Mifflin, 1991.

———. *Preachers of Hate: Islam and the War on America.* New York: Crown, 2003.

Trainor, Bernard, and Michael Gordon. *The General's War: The Inside Story of the Conflict in the Gulf.* Boston: Little, Brown, 1995.
Zinsmeister, Karl. *Boots on the Ground.* New York: St. Martin's Press, 2003.

FICTION
Hirsh, M. E. *Kabul.* New York: Griffin Trade Books, 2002.
Hosseini, Khalid. *The Kite Runner.* New York: Riverhead Books, 2003.
Mendes, Bob. *Vengeance: Prelude to Saddam's War.* Trans. by H. S. Smittenaar. Fairfax Station, Va.: Intercontinental Publishing, 2000.
Michener, James. *Caravans: A Novel of Afghanistan.* New York: Random House, 2003.
Shah, Idries. *Kara Kush: A Novel of Afghanistan.* Woodstock, N.Y.: Overlook Press, 2002.
Wilson, Steven. *Winter in Kandahar.* Shaker Heights, Ohio: Hailey-Grey Books, 2003.

VHS/DVD
Afghanistan—the Vicious Circle (1999). Nima Film, VHS, 1999.
Afghan Stories (2002). Vanguard Cinema, DVD, 2003.
America 9/11—We Will Never Forget (2001). Spectrum Film, DVD, 2001.
America Remembers (2002). CNN/Wea Corp, DVD, 2002.
Caravans (1978). Jef Films, VHS, 2003.
Escape from Afghanistan (2002). New Concorde Home Video, DVD, 2003.
Frontline: In Search of bin Laden (2001). PBS Home Video, VHS, 2001.
New Faces of Terrorism (2000). A&E Entertainment, VHS, 2000.
9/11—the Filmmakers' Commemorative Edition (2002). Paramount Home Video, DVD, 2002.
Secrets of the Gulf War (1998). Image Entertainment, DVD, 2001.
Three Kings (1999). Warner Home Video, VHS/DVD, 2003.
21 Days to Baghdad (2003) National Geographic/Warner Homer video, DVD, 2003.
Uncle Saddam (2003). Xenon Entertainment, VHS/DVD, 2003.
War in Iraq—the Road to Baghdad (2003). CNN/Wea Corp, VHS/DVD, 2003.

WEBSITES
"Blix Report to UN Security Council." washingtonpost.com. Available online. URL http://www.washingtonpost.com/wp-dyn/articles/A49612-2003Jan27.html. Posted on January 27, 2003.
Bush, George W. "State of the Union Address, January 28, 2003." University of Michigan Documents Center. Available online. URL: http://www.lib. umich.edu/govdocs/text/su2003.txt. Downloaded on August 7, 2003.

CNN.com. "Arab Voices: Where's Saddam and Who's Next?" April 16, 2003. Available online. URL: http://www.cnn.com/2003/WORLD/meast/04/16/sprj.irq.arab.voices/index/html. Downloaded on April 17, 2003.

Commonwealth Institute. "War Report—Iraq War and Afghan Aftermath." Available online. URL: http://www.comw.org/warreport/iraqarchive1.html. Downloaded on December 11, 2003.

The Economist. "Iraq's Rising Price Tag." Economist.com. Available online. URL: http://www.economist.com/agenda/displayStory.cfm?story_id=2049581. Downloaded on December 11, 2003.

Escobar, Pepe. "Fear and Anger in the Sunni Triangle." Asia Times Online. Available online. URL: http://www.atimes.com/atimes/Middle_East/E130Ak01.html. Posted on September 30, 2003.

Global Policy Forum. "Iraq Crisis." Available online. URL: http://www.globalpolicy.org/security/issues/iraqindx.htm. Downloaded on December 11, 2003.

Globalsecurity.org. "Operation Enduring Freedom." Available online. URL: http://www.globalsecurity.org/military/ops/enduring-freedom-ops.htm. Downloaded on September 12, 2003.

McGeary, Johanna. "Dissecting the Case." Time Online Edition. Available online. URL: http://www.time.com/time/magazine/printout/08816,418519,00.html. Posted on February 10, 2003.

Prusher, Ilene R. "U.S. Antiguerrilla Campaign Draws Iraqi Ire." The Christian Science Monitor. Available online. URL: http://www.csmonitor.com/2003/0616/p10s01-woiq.htm. Downloaded on December 11, 2003.

New York Times. "Report by the Chief Inspector for Biological and Chemical Arms." The New York Times on the Web. Available online. URL: http://www.nytimes.com/2003/02/14/international/middleeast/14/WEB_BTEX.html. Downloaded on February 19, 2003.

REGIMENTS.ORG. "Iraq War 2003." Available online. URL: http://www.regiments.org/milhist/wars21stcent/03iraq.htm. Downloaded on December 11, 2003.

Reuters. "Canada Rules Out Joining Solo U.S. Attack on Iraq." The New York Times on the Web. Available online. URL: http://www.nytimes.com/reuters/international/international-iraq-canada.html. Downloaded on February 19, 2003.

———. "Iraqi Scientist Says Saddam Hiding Arms Underground." The New York Times on the Web. Available online. URL: http://www.nytimes.com/reuters/international/international-iraq-philippines-scientist.html. Downloaded on February 19, 2003.

———. "U.N. Criticizes Iraq over Scientist Interviews." The New York Times on the Web. Available online. URL: http://www.nytimes.com/reuters/international/international-iraq-inspectors.html. Downloaded on February 19, 2003.

Sharkey, Jacqueline E. "The Television War." Available online. URL: http://www.ajr.org/article_printable.asp?id=2988. Downloaded on December 11, 2003.

US News and World Report. "Making the Case for War." USNews.com. Available online. URL: http://www.usnews.com/usnews/issue/030210/usnews/10war.htm. Downloaded on February 5, 2003.

White House News Release. "President Says Saddam Hussein Must Leave Iraq within 48 Hours." Available online. URL: http://www.whitehouse.gov/news/releases/2003/03.htm. Downloaded on August 7, 2003.

Index

Page numbers in *italic* indicate photographs. Page numbers followed by *m* indicate maps. Page numbers followed by *g* indicate glossary entries. Page numbers in **boldface** indicate box features.

INDEX